SPACE
THE WHOLE WHIZZ-BANG STORY

Glenn Murphy wrote his first book, *Why Is Snot Green?*, while working at the Science Museum, London. Since then he has written around twenty popular science titles aimed at kids and teens, including the bestselling *How Loud Can You Burp?* and *A Kids' Guide to Global Warming*.

His books are read by brainy children, parents and teachers worldwide, and have been translated into Dutch, German, Spanish, Turkish, Finnish, Chinese, Japanese, Korean and Indonesian. Which is kind of awesome. In 2007 he moved to the United States and began writing full-time, which explains why he now says things like 'kind of awesome'.

These days he lives in sunny, leafy North Carolina – with his wife Heather, his son Sean, and two *unfeasibly* large felines.

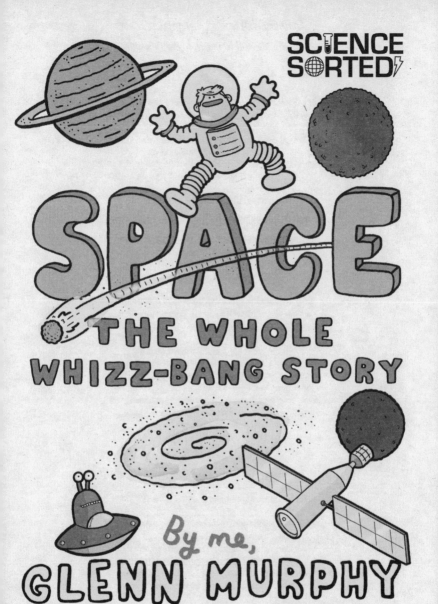

SCIENCE SORTED

SPACE

THE WHOLE WHIZZ-BANG STORY

By me,

GLENN MURPHY

Illustrated by Mike Phillips

MACMILLAN CHILDREN'S BOOKS

*To Henry Walker – a truly great teacher,
and inspiration to many. Myself included.*

Some material in this book has previously been published in 2010
by Macmillan Children's Books in *Space, Black Holes and Stuff*

This edition published 2013 by Macmillan Children's Books
a division of Macmillan Publishers Limited
20 New Wharf Road, London N1 9RR
Basingstoke and Oxford
Associated companies throughout the world
www.panmacmillan.com

ISBN 978-1-4472-2623-9

A CIP catalogue record for this book is available from the British Library.

Printed and bound by CPI Group (UK) Ltd, Croydon CR0 4YY

PICTURE CREDITS

Pages 28 Shutterstock/ Panos Karas; 33 Claudius Ptolemäus, Picture of 16th century book
frontispiece / Wikipedia; 38 Shutterstock/ Nicku; 41 Shutterstock/ Nicku; 44 Shutterstock/
Nicku; 49 Shutterstock/ Giorgois Kollidas; 54 Wikipedia; 80 NASA; 81 NASA/Apollo Program;
82/83 Shutterstock/ Petr Jilek; 124 NASA/Mars Exploration Program; 140 Shutterstock/ Nicku;
141 NASA/JPL; 177 Shutterstock/ LingHK

CONTENTS

Hang on a Minute – What Is the Universe?

That is a very, very good question. One that most people don't bother to ask.

The Universe is *all there is.* Literally.

EVERYTHING. All of it.

It contains everything from
vast galaxies,
stars,
black holes,
planets,
moons,
oceans,
rivers,
lakes,
land masses

. . . plus every single life-form that lives on (or in) them.

All there is? Like, EVERYTHING?

Yep. *Everything*. The word 'universe' comes from the Greek, meaning 'all together' or 'turned into one'. And as far as we know there's nothing beyond it. Cosmologists reckon it's billions of light years across and, since it's still expanding, it's getting bigger every day.

We also know that it's around 13.7 billion years old, and began life in a huge explosion of matter and energy known as the ...

Big Bang!

(They must have been up all night thinking up the name for that one.)

Before that there was nothing. No matter, no energy . . . no
Space, even. The Bang created all these things as it went.

Get it Sorted – Light Year

A light year is the distance travelled by a particle of light,
moving at the speed of light, in one Earth year. Since the speed
of light is roughly 300 million metres per second (or 670 million
miles per hour), that means a light year is roughly equal to about
9,500,000,000,000 (nine trillion, five hundred billion) kilometres, or
5,900,000,000,000 (five trillion, nine hundred million) miles.
Or, put another way, 63,000 times the distance
from the Earth to the Sun.

Now multiply that by
27,400,000,000, and that'll
give you some idea of how big
the Universe is (or at least
the small part of it we can
see – it's very probably much
bigger!)

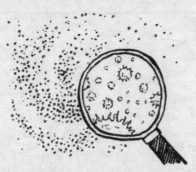

BIG NUMBERS ALERT!

We know that the Universe contains over 100 billion galaxies.
Within each galaxy at least 70,000 million million million (or
70 sextillion) stars happily twinkle. Well, not so much twinkle
as BURN.

Stars burn?

Yep. And, what's more, they burn brighter and hotter than
anything on Earth. Stars, we've discovered, are not little
twinkling dots in the dark curtain of the sky.

They are massive, ball-shaped nuclear reactors — giant spheres of hydrogen and helium gas burning and exploding with energy from nuclear reactions going on within them.

Yikes. That sounds a bit scary, actually. Massive nuclear reactors. Like . . . how massive?

Well, our own star — the Sun — is roughly 109 times wider than the Earth, and 330,000 times heavier. And that's not even one of the big ones. Some stars are 100 to 1,000 times wider *again*. They can get so massive, in fact, that they collapse in on themselves, then rebound with an explosion that burns a billion times brighter than the Sun – leaving behind an enormous, invisible hole in Space from which nothing can escape. What's more, a monstrous black hole like this could lie at the centre of our own galaxy, the Milky Way.

Get it Sorted – How Big is the Universe?

Unlike galaxies and solar systems, the Universe has no single central point, and may have no edge. Physicists say it's quite possible that the Universe simply folds back on itself. So if you flew a spaceship in one direction for long enough, you would never actually reach the edge of the Universe. Just like flying an aeroplane around the world, you'd end up back where you started. Only billions of years older, and probably quite annoyed.

But how do you KNOW all this stuff? I mean, it's not like you can jet about in Space with a huge ruler, measuring the stars and the distances between them, is it?

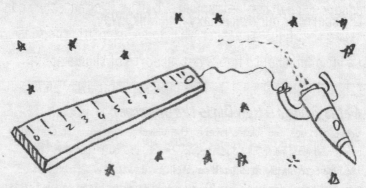

Again — great question. The answer is: we use science.

Science isn't just a collection of clever facts and figures. It's a way — an incredibly clever and useful way — of figuring things out using not only careful measurements, but also theories, tests and experiments. So while. . .

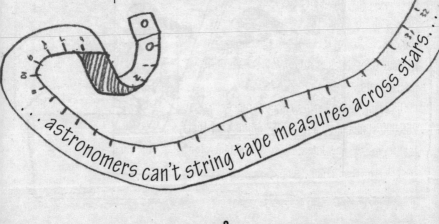

. . . astronomers can't string tape measures across stars. . .

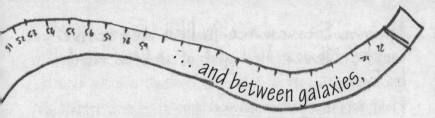

... and between galaxies,

they can measure the light that comes from them, using telescopes and other instruments. Believe it or not, they can then use that light (together with some scientific theories and a bit of maths) to figure out all sorts of things about the thing it came from. Like how large, how far away and what kind of star it is. Often they can even tell what it's made of and how old it is — all from one tiny speck of light! Like police detectives working with tiny scraps of evidence, scientists can piece together an entire story from bits and pieces that seem to mean nothing.

Early Greek astronomer and mathematician Erastosthenes (276–195 BC) successfully calculated the width and circumference of the Earth, the tilt of the Earth's axis and the distance from the Earth to the Sun, all without telescopes or other modern scientific instruments.

His crack at the Earth's circumference was 250,000 stadia, or about 39,700 kilometres. The real figure, we now know, is around 40,000 kilometres. Not too shabby for a scientist working 2,000 years ago!

Hmmm. So science is like detective work? Never thought of it like that before . . .

Right. And that's what makes science such an exciting and powerful thing to learn about. It's not just a collection of facts to be learned. It's a method. And you can use it yourself to find out more about the world around you, just as working scientists do every day. We'll be doing plenty of that, and discovery and detective work, right here.

So where do we start?

We'll kick off with a look at astronomy itself. We'll see when and where it began, and how it developed to a science that has allowed us to send men to the Moon, roving robots to Mars and Space probes to Saturn and beyond.

From there, we're off on a whirlwind tour of our own solar system, complete with planets, moons, comets and asteroid belts. We'll learn what Saturn's rings are made of, why Uranus rolls sideways around the solar system and why poor old Pluto doesn't get to be a planet any more.

If that sounds like fun to you, then grab your Space boots and star map, as we're off to get Space SORTED!

IT'S IN THE STARS

What is astronomy?

Astronomers study the stars to increase our knowledge of the Universe.

So how far back does all this stargazing go?

You might be surprised to find out that the roots of astronomy go *waaaaay* back, and that people all over the world have been stargazing since ancient times.

But how did they do it without telescopes and instruments and stuff?

Well, we'll get to that in a minute. But basically they started by just looking at the stars, and spotting patterns in the sky that would tell them things.

Like what kind of week they were gonna have, who they would meet and stuff like that? Like reading the 'stars' in the paper? My mum does that.

Ah. Not quite. That's not really *astronomy*, you see — that's *astrology*.

Get it Sorted – Astronomy vs Astrology

Celestial objects are objects found outside the Earth's atmosphere, such as galaxies, stars, planets, moons and comets. They're usually viewed in the night sky, though some are also visible during the day.

Astronomy is the scientific study of celestial objects and Space, which uses careful observations and theories of physics, chemistry and mathematics to explain how the Universe works.

Astrology is a non-scientific practice which centres around the belief that the movement of rocks and gas balls in Space directly affects the personal lives of people on Earth. So, if Venus moves between the Earth and a certain group of distant stars, then love waits behind a green door (possibly wearing a black hat)'. If Mars and Mercury line up, it's a bad day to travel'. And so on.

Whether or not you believe astrology is up to you.

Where did the first astronomers come from?

Lots of cultures helped to develop it. The ancient Babylonians, Egyptians and Greeks had perhaps the first advanced stargazing systems, while in the Middle Ages scholars in Asia and the Middle East made huge contributions to astronomy as a modern science.

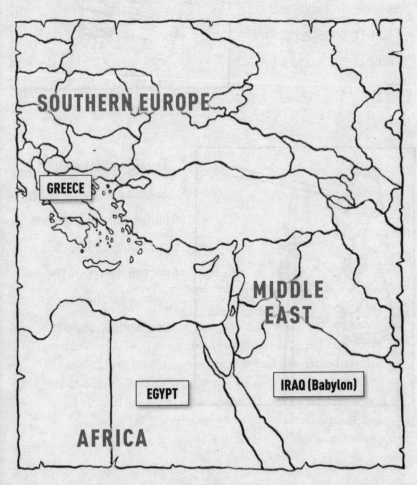

The **Babylonians** lived over 5,000 years ago. They were very skilled mathematicians, and they kept detailed records of sunrises and sunsets that allowed them to construct some of the world's first calendars.

The **Egyptians** charted star constellations and built their magnificent pyramids to line up, at certain times of the year, with the stars' positions in the sky.

In the first century AD, the ancient **Greeks** were coming up with models of how the Sun, Moon, planets and stars moved around. And while they weren't quite right — more about that in a minute — they did pave the way for better attempts (and more accurate models) later on.

Chinese astronomers created some of the world's first whole-sky star maps, and kept measurements accurate enough to build clocks, predict eclipses, track comets and more.

So did they just figure all this stuff out for themselves?

Yes and no. While the ancient Babylonians and Egyptians probably kicked it all off, the Greeks borrowed and improved upon their ideas. And, later still, the Arabs gathered together works from ancient Greece and China and added knowledge of their own. Not many people know it, but we owe much of our astronomical knowledge to the Arab peoples.

Why did people think the Sun went around the Earth? Were they stupid or something?

For a while, an Earth-centred solar system was easier to imagine and seemed to make more sense. After all — the Sun and Moon seemed to move across the sky and around the Earth, and the Earth didn't seem to be moving through Space, so why not put it in the middle?

These days, astronomers know a lot about Space, stars, solar systems and planets. You probably know quite a bit about them yourself. Let's find out.

The astronomical Arabs

In the Islamic world, the tribes and peoples had their own long history of stargazing. This was, at first, partly for navigating the deserts where they lived (which had few landmarks on the ground, but countless ones overhead in the cloudless, starry skies). But later it was for judging the right time and direction to face for Islamic prayer times.

The Islamic scholars translated ancient Greek writings, and adapted their ideas and instruments to produce calendars and star-charts of their own. Scholars like Abd Allah Muhammad Ibn Jabir Sinan al-Battani wrote and rewrote many important works on astrology, and started to draw out the differences between astrology, used for fortune-telling, and astronomy as a pure and accurate study of 'the heavens' for its own sake. It was this idea – and these works – that went on to influence the European scholars who later popularized astronomy as a modern science.

Have a look at the four sentences below, and think about how you would respond to hearing them.

 The Sun is in the middle of our solar system.

☆ The Earth and all the other planets move around it.

☆ The Earth also spins or rotates on its own axis, making one full turn per day.

☆ This makes the Sun, Moon and stars seem to rotate or move across the sky.

Now – what was your response to each one?
Was it:

a) No way. Don't believe you.

b) Really?? I had no idea . . .

c) Duhhhhhh. Tell me something I don't know.

Duhhhhhh!!
Everyone
knows
the Earth
goes around
the Sun.
So (c).

Right. Almost everyone these days would answer (c). All this seems pretty obvious to us now.

But it wasn't *always* that way.

But that's just stupid! Weren't very clever, these scholars, were they?

Well, all this might seem strange (or just plain daft) now. But if you think about it, these ideas kind of make sense.

Eh?

After all, each day, the Sun rises in the east, moves across the sky, and sets in the west. So does the Moon — although we can't always see it doing so.

And if you watch the stars at night for long enough you'll notice that they seem to move too. So it really *looks* like everything is circling us, and that we're staying still.

And if you really think about it, unless someone *told* you the Earth was spinning and circling, why would you think it was?

Errr . . . I'm not following you. What do you mean?

Think about it. You can't *feel* the Earth moving. So where's your evidence for it?

WHOOOOOOOH!

Hmmm. Now that I think about it . . . you're right.

And this is roughly what people argued for most of astronomical history. And part of the reason why few people believed that the Earth went round the Sun (and not the other way around) until about 400 years ago.

People believed that? For that long?

Yep. *That* long. After the . . .

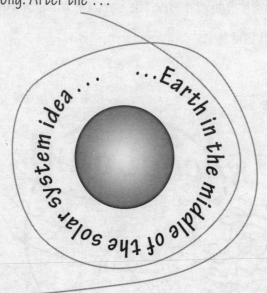

. . . **Earth in the middle of the solar system idea** . . .

. . . was suggested by Aristotle, Ptolemy and other scholars in ancient Greece, it stuck around for more than a millennium.

While a few people (even in ancient Greece) argued otherwise, they were soon shouted down by other scholars and religious leaders. As a result, almost no one believed in a Sun-centred solar system — right up until the sixteenth century.

Why? What happened then?

It was then that the real battle for the stars would begin. A battle that would change the course of scientific history. And the battleground was Europe.

Are you sitting comfortably? Good. Then let's begin the tale . . .

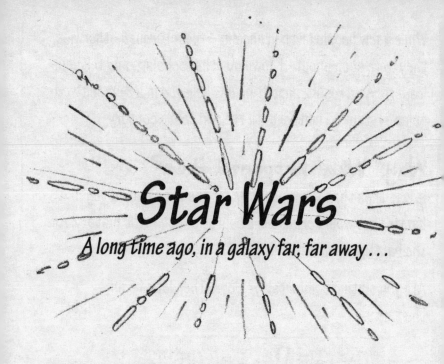

Star Wars

A long time ago, in a galaxy far, far away . . .

All right, so it wasn't that long ago. And it was . . . well . . . right here. This galaxy. This planet.

GET. ON. WITH. IT.

Sorry. Now where was I? Oh, yeah. (*Ahem.*)

The battle for the stars raged between two camps.

On one side, there was the huge army of scholars, religious leaders and ordinary folk who believed that the Earth was in the middle of everything. This is called the Geocentric (or 'Earth-centred') model of the solar system. The Middle-Earth army ruled the world from ancient times right up to the late 1500s and beyond.

On the other side were the few philosophers, mathematicians and other scholars who believed that the Earth and other planets circled the Sun. This was called the Heliocentric (or 'Sun-centred') model of the solar system. From the 1500s onwards, the Sun-Centred Rebels started building their numbers and began their battle to be heard.

But it wasn't easy. As with most wars, each side believed their ideas made the most sense, and neither army was giving up without a fight. Heroes emerged on both sides of the battle, and there are too many to tell of them all. But here are some of the big names and big thinkers who helped to start, fight and settle the argument.

Aristotle: the Earth and the heavens

Aristotle (384– 322 BC) was a Greek philosopher and all-round **genius**. He not only studied and wrote some of the earliest

works on astronomy, physics and biology, he was also a musician, a poet and a politician. He set the tone for the whole astronomical argument by offering a clever – and very popular – explanation of how the Sun, planets and stars fitted together.

To Aristotle, the Universe was divided into two major bits —

the Earth
the heavens

The Earth, where we live, was imperfect and a bit disordered. But the heavens — lofty home of the Sun, the stars, the planets and the gods — were perfect.

Perfect?

Yes. Perfect. Or so Aristotle, and his many followers, believed. He came up with a model of the Universe in which the Earth was surrounded by about fifty rotating (and presumably see-through) spherical shells.

Eh? Bit weird, isn't it?

It is a bit. I suppose it'd look a little like one of those Russian dolls, where smaller shells fit inside bigger and bigger ones. Only instead of dolls picture a multi-sized set of enormous transparent footballs. That should do it.

Anyway, in Aristotle's model, the Earth sat, unmoving, in the very centre. Outside that was the innermost shell (or celestial sphere, as he called them) which housed the Moon. This was somehow lodged into the wall of the invisible shell, so as the shell turned the Moon turned with it. Hence, the Moon went round the Earth, as everyone could clearly see. Made perfect sense to him.

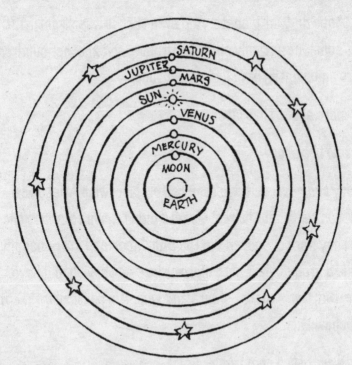

Riiight ... Perfect sense ...

Outside that shell or sphere was another one, this time carrying Mercury. The next carried Venus, and the one after that, the Sun. From there, you had spheres carrying Jupiter, Saturn and the 'fixed stars'. And that was it.

But what about the rest of the planets? Like Neptune, and Pluto?

Well, Uranus, Neptune and Pluto hadn't been discovered yet. Astronomers had to wait another 2,000 years, for the invention of the telescope, before anyone could even hope to see those distant planets. And even then it wasn't until 1781 that someone actually spotted Uranus, and another hundred years again until they clocked Neptune.

But more about that later.

Back to the story.

Pretty and neat as it was, the *real* problem with Aristotle's Universe was that the real planets didn't seem to *behave* the way they were supposed to. The Sun, Moon and stars happily rotated around the Earth more or less as they should have done. But the planets – Mars and Venus, in particular – kept misbehaving.

They were often spotted moving 'backwards' through the heavens (something astronomers later called 'retrograde motion') as if their particular celestial spheres had slowed down, sped up or changed direction.

Still – Aristotle's model was as good an explanation as any for how the Universe worked. And, for a while at least, no one could do better. Until, that is, Ptolemy hit the scene.

Ptolemy: now here's us in the middle . . .

Claudius Ptolemy (AD 150) came up with a way of explaining those mischievous wandering planets.

The word 'planet' comes from a Greek word meaning 'wanderer' – which goes to show you how much of a problem this was.

So how did he do that? Did he put the Sun in the middle, where it's supposed to be?

Nope. Ptolemy's model still had the Earth in the middle, but instead of having the planets stuck on simple spheres, he had them moving in circles on top of circles. So Mars would orbit a point in Space, which in turn would orbit the Earth. If you followed its path, it looked more like it was looping or bouncing around the Earth than simply lapping it.

Ptolemy's head-spinning Universe

Ptolemy solved the 'wandering planet' problem by adding epicycles (or circles on top of circles) to some of the planets' orbits. It sort of worked, but it got pretty twisty and complicated!

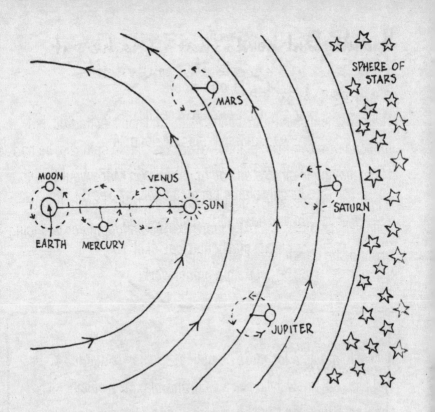

What? Why would anyone believe that? It's so crazy and complicated it'd never work.

Right. But remember that back then people didn't know any different — or rather didn't have many other ideas to compare it to. What's more, believe it or not, Ptolemy's model more or less *worked*.

It did? But how?

Convinced that circles were the way forward (since Aristotle had stated that the circle was the only shape 'perfect' enough to be in the heavens), Ptolemy used his great mathematical skill to *make* his model work.

In truth, it was a lot more complicated than it needed to be, and the real answer to the wandering-planet problem — that the Earth just isn't in the middle — was a lot simpler.

So why didn't the other astronomers just figure that out?

Because Ptolemy's model seemed to fit what astronomers were seeing well enough, and everyone felt happy that the...

Earth was the *centre of all things*.

They felt that this was how it *should* be. Hence, this Ptolemaic model of the Universe was widely accepted as the 'right' one, and it stood largely unchallenged for over 1,300 years. (Not at all bad, as theories go.)

Until someone else came along and put it all right . . . right?

Right. It was at this point that the rebels joined the battle in force — led by a Polish astronomer and maths whizz determined to stir up the solar system.

Copernicus

Copernicus: Sun-centred circles

Nicolaus Copernicus (1473–1543) wasn't the first person to suggest the Earth went around the Sun. But thanks to his work many more people became convinced that it *made more sense* that way.

He did all the maths, drew all the pictures and wrote an extremely important book arguing for a Sun-centred solar system. His book was called *De Revolutionibus Orbium Celestium,* meaning 'Of the Circling Celestial

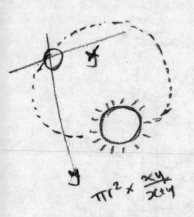

Spheres'. But his pattern of moving sky-spheres was very different to that of Aristotle.

In Copernicus's solar system, the Sun sat in the middle, with Mercury, Venus, Earth, Mars, Jupiter and Saturn circling around it. The Moon, he said, was alone in circling the Earth, and the 'fixed stars' still sat outside the whole arrangement. Sound familiar? It should, as it's more or less how we know the planets to be arranged, even today.

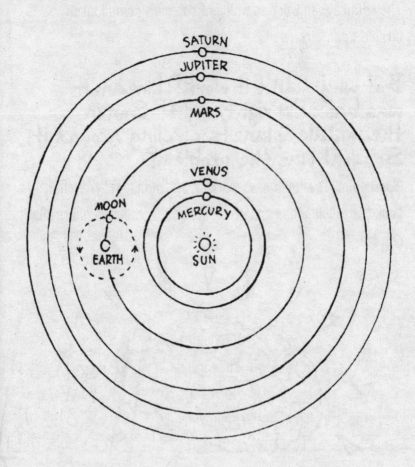

So everyone went for it, and Copernicus won the battle, right?

Errr . . . not quite. You see, there was a problem with Copernicus's Sun-centred circles. They didn't quite work.

What?!

They didn't even work as well as Ptolemy's complicated circles-upon-circles did.

But why didn't it work? I mean, it was basically right, right? Sun in the middle, planets circling around it? So what was the problem?

Good point. It should have worked, but didn't. Why? Well, it took the intelligence and precision of a German to figure that one out . . .

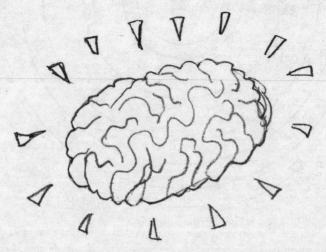

Kepler: ovals for orbits

Johannes Kepler (1571–1630) was a German mathematician and astronomer who sussed out, among other things, the nature of Copernicus's problem.

So what was it?

Basically this: Copernicus was right to argue that the planets circle the Sun, rather than the Earth. But he was wrong in thinking they move in *circles*. Because they don't.

They don't?

Nope.

Planets actually orbit the Sun in flattened circles, otherwise known as ovals or ellipses.

By trying to keep Aristotle's perfect heavenly circles and spheres, Copernicus – like Aristotle – had come up with a beautiful, neat model that the planets simply refused to follow. Once Kepler had figured this out and tried using ellipses *instead* of circles, everything started falling into place.

His Sun-centred, oval-orbit model of the solar system didn't just work better than those of Ptolemy and Copernicus – it worked perfectly. Kepler even figured out how to calculate the path and speed of each planet's orbit based on how far it was from the Sun. His three Laws of Planetary Motion, which tell us how to do this, still stand today.

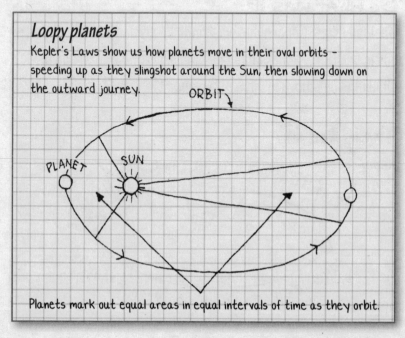

Loopy planets

Kepler's Laws show us how planets move in their oval orbits – speeding up as they slingshot around the Sun, then slowing down on the outward journey.

ORBIT

PLANET   SUN

Planets mark out equal areas in equal intervals of time as they orbit.

So that was it, then? Solar system sorted. Problem solved.

Sadly, no. Not *just* yet.

While Kepler's tweaks to Copernicus's Sun-centred system worked a treat, many (or most) people still refused to believe the Earth wasn't sitting, neat and still, in the centre of the Universe.

So the battle raged on, and still more heroes of astronomy lined up to fight it . . .

Galileo: look, it moves!

Galileo Galilei (1564–1642) was one of those heroes, and although he didn't win the battle outright, the arguments and evidence he put forward helped tip the odds in favour of the Sun-centred rebellion.

Galileo, an Italian mathematician, philosopher and engineer, built some of the world's earliest (but not the very first) telescopes. More importantly, he was one of the first people to use telescopes to make detailed, accurate observations of the planets and stars.

He saw sunspots on the Sun, mountains on the Moon and was puzzled by the 'ears' he spotted on Saturn.

(We now know they were Saturn's rings, but he wasn't to know that!)

But what difference did that make?

Not much, at first. But then he turned his telescope on Jupiter. There, Galileo discovered four moons orbiting around it.

So what? So Jupiter had moons. Big deal.

Ahh — but it *was* a big deal. Back then, you see, the only planet known to have a moon was ours — the Earth. This was one of the arguments the Middle-Earth scholars used to defend their model. 'Everything goes around us,' they argued, 'and nothing goes around anything else. Therefore, we must be the perfect centre of everything.'

But now Jupiter *did* have something going around it.
Four things, in fact.

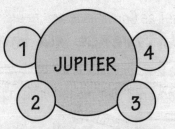

Oops. Looks like we **weren't** the centre of *everything*, after all.

Jupiter's multi-moons

Jupiter actually has at least sixty-three moons, most of which were discovered in the last few years! Galileo discovered the first four in 1610, and between then and 1999, ten more were found, bringing the total to fourteen. Then, between 2000 and 2003, astronomers spotted another thirty-two moons, and they're still going!

See page 136 for more about Jupiter's moons

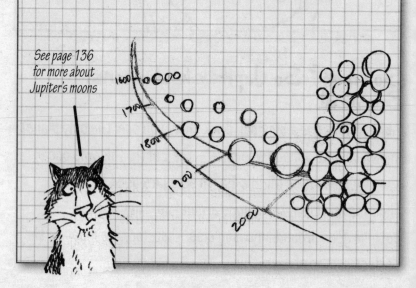

For this and other reasons, Galileo argued that the Sun *was* clearly in the centre of the solar system, and the Earth *did* move around it, just as Copernicus and Kepler had described. And he wrote and published books saying so.

... and everyone read them, and AT LAST the battle was over. Right?

Errr, no. Sorry.

Argh!! Why not?

Well, for one thing, most people at that time didn't know how to read. For another, Galileo's books didn't go down too well with most religious leaders in Europe. They felt that saying the Earth *wasn't* the perfect centre of everything was blasphemy — like mocking the Bible and God. The Catholic

Church arrested and threatened Galileo, and forced him to apologize in public, saying that he lied and that the Earth doesn't move at all. But in true rebel style, it's said that he mumbled, 'Nevertheless, it moves,' under his breath right afterwards.

Heh, heh. Nice work. But if he didn't sort it all out, then who did?

Well, no one person sorted the whole thing. But if one guy could take the credit for convincing the most people, it would probably be the famous British hero of science, Sir Isaac Newton.

Newton: here's why it moves ... gravity

Sir Isaac Newton (1642–1727) built on Galileo's groundwork, and delivered what was to be the final blow to the Middle-Earth army.

Going far beyond all other models before him, Newton was a mathematical **genius** who figured out – among a gazillion other things – what makes planets orbit the Sun.

And the answer to that puzzle was

GRAVITY

Gravity is a force that attracts everything in the Universe to everything else.

The bigger and closer together any two things are, the more attraction there is between them. Stars, planets and moons are about as big as it gets.

So...

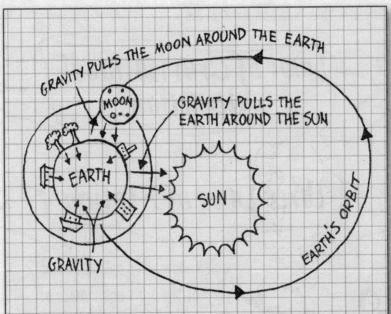

GRAVITY PULLS THE MOON AROUND THE EARTH

GRAVITY PULLS THE EARTH AROUND THE SUN

MOON

EARTH

SUN

GRAVITY

EARTH'S ORBIT

- We (along with the atmosphere, oceans, trees, three-toed sloths and everything else) are held to the surface of the Earth by the attractive pull of gravity
- The Moon is pulled into orbit around the Earth by their combined gravitational attraction
- And the Earth is pulled into orbit around the Sun by their combined gravitational force too.

This neatly solved the problem of why we can't feel the Earth moving — the air moves with us, because it's stuck to the Earth too, so it doesn't rush past us as we move through Space. But, more importantly, it also explained why the smaller planets would orbit a larger Sun, rather than the other way around.

Beyond, this, Newton gave us his

Laws of Gravitational Attraction

and his

Three Laws of Motion

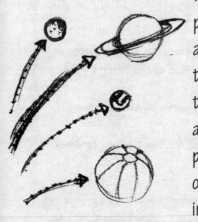

which allow us to calculate and predict the orbit and motion of almost any object — be it planet, tennis ball, moon or missile — in the Universe. Using his laws and equations, he successfully predicted the positions and motions of all the planets then known to be in the solar system. What's more, a century later, astronomers used the same laws to predict where Neptune should be (and found it within hours of turning their telescopes to that part of the sky).

Armed with his theories, laws and explanations, Newton made it difficult for the remaining Middle-Earth scholars to protest. They'd simply run out of objections. Newton's explanation of the solar system not only told us **how** it behaved, but also **why** it behaved that way — because of <u>GRAVITY</u>. Beyond that, his equations predicted precisely where planets would be, and never seemed to be wrong. Hard to top that.

So that was it? Newton nailed it, and now we use his ideas because he's never been topped?

Yes. Well, kind of. While the battle for the shape of the solar system was pretty much won, there was perhaps one more guy who went beyond Newton.

Perhaps the most famous scientist in history.

Yep — you guessed it. It was Albert Einstein.

Einstein: but what is gravity?

Albert Einstein (1879–1955) was a German office worker and amateur physicist when he came up with an idea that would change our view of the Universe once and for all. If anyone can be said to have topped Newton, it's him.

Einstein's work was pure **genius**, and to tell you everything about what it means would take at least ten more books like this one. But he gets an honorary mention here,

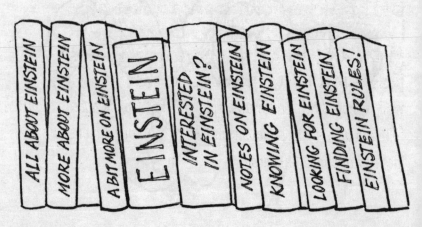

because his General Theory of Relativity provided the final evidence for a Sun-centred solar system, and proved once and for all that Copernicus, Kepler, Galileo and everyone else who had argued for it were right all along.

Einstein's work told us not only how **GRAVITY** works (as Newton's did), but also *what* **GRAVITY** *is*.

Gravity is a warping or folding of Space around any object in the Universe.

And the more massive the object, the more warping there is.

Eh? But how can Space fold up? I mean, it's ... well ... Space. You can't bend it or crumple it. It's just kind of ... there. Right?

Well, it's pretty hard for us to picture, but Space *does* in fact fold and bend like a sheet. It just does it in four dimensions, instead of the usual three.

Errr ... four dimensions? You've lost me there.

Einstein believed that three-dimensional Space and the extra dimension of time formed parts of the same thing — a four-dimensional 'fabric' called space–time. Gravity, said Einstein, is a warping of space–time.

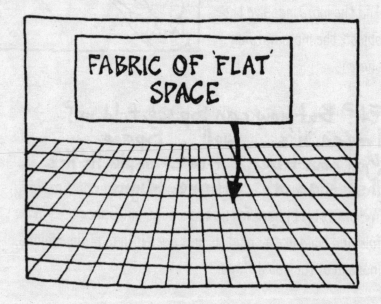

FABRIC OF 'FLAT' SPACE

Try this. Imagine the Sun as a giant basketball placed on a huge, flat sheet (the fabric of space—time), and the planets as tennis balls and golf balls placed alongside it.

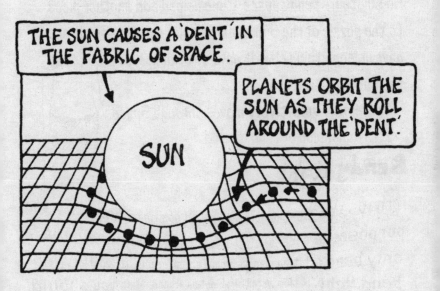

The weight (or mass) of the ball puts a dent into the sheet, and any object close enough to the dent will roll in, following the warping or curving of the dent around the ball. Roll a golf ball past the basketball, and it'll start rolling in circles around the dent. And that's similar to how planets orbit suns (and moons orbit planets) in Space.

Knowing this helps explain why planets would bother to orbit the Sun in the first place (rather than, say, just be pulled straight into it by the force of Newton's famous gravity). So Einstein's bendy space—time helped add another piece to the puzzle of the Sun-centred solar system. But it also gave us something else. It gave us evidence, or proof, that the Earth...

...definitely, **positively** moves through Space.

Bendy light

Perhaps the most important part of Einstein's theory, for the purposes of our story, is that his warping gravity would not only bend orbiting planets around massive suns, it would also bend **light**. If this were true, Einstein argued, then you should be able to see a tiny shift in the position of a star behind the Sun when the Sun moves between us and that star. The light from it will literally bend around the Sun, and will seem to be in a different spot, relative to the other stars around it.

But – duhhh – you can't see stars when the Sun's out. That means it's DAYTIME.

Right. Unfortunately, we can't usually see stars close to the Sun (or even anywhere near it), since the Sun shines so much brighter and bounces off the atmosphere, obscuring the fainter light from the stars beyond. *That's* why we can't see stars during the daytime, and why the first ones only appear as the Sun is setting.

See. Told you.

But fortunately there is one time when we can see stars close to the Sun. That's during a solar eclipse.

In an eclipse, the Moon moves between the Earth and the Sun, shading a region of the Earth from its rays, and darkening the skies. Stars are visible during the daytime, and astronomers can look at them — even stars close to the Sun itself.

And that, in 1919, is what scientist and adventurer Sir Arthur Eddington did. He led two expeditions across the world just to be in the right place during an eclipse, so that his team of astronomers could turn their telescopes on to stars near the Sun. When they did so, they noticed just what Einstein had predicted – the stars had shifted. Which meant the light was bent, and Einstein's Space-bending gravity was real.

Hurrah! Einstein's Space-bending gravity is real!!

Hooray! FINALLY. Victory to the rebels!

Yep. Finally. By this time, as I said before, the battle was pretty much already over. Most people had long since accepted the Sun-centred solar system, and Newton's theories of gravity and gravitation. But Einstein's work nailed it once and for all. We not only knew what the Universe looked like, and how it behaved, we also knew *why* it behaved that way.

And somewhere along the way real, proper science was born.

Astronomer wordsearch

Can you find these words hidden in the grid? They may be horizontal, vertical or diagonal.

Aristotle	Gravity	Ellipse	Newton
Einstein	Kepler	Ptolemy	Orbit
Copernicus	Heliocentric	Geocentric	

```
K U S K F Z J H Y C A B N D F V N J K A
X R F C C X C A E G X E T E V G Z E Y H
O R K O T H H P U L U U C S W M B N Q V
L H K Z I D D E O J I B G O O T K H O X
D V K B C I R T N E C O E G O E O N G A
A M D A N T P U S V C Q C H D L L N X A
R S U C I N R E P O C D L E R T P K N S
U F R I E R X D A Y H W F K N O T V R P
U L X O T B J B W M U H V E S T Q W S W
N T W C S W P W J E I X T P N S R I L T
P N H X N I V Y H L O W K L S I V I X Y
Q E Y T I V A R G O X B D E V R I X C O
K M S C E I R B N T I I M R F A I V X D
O D H P K P Z N C P H R N F W S C M B A
B Q J T I F E Z C J U J C P P O M N J O
D L U E O L U X J O H Q H U M Q V T M G
W U U T R N L Z W X E L X Z E Z J V I W
C E J R B F P E U G P H T G Q X S D M I
N X F A I P T A M Q M C B B U E S Q G O
F R V R T B Y J D I X A J D K K C T J I
```

Answers on page 188

A TRIP AROUND THE SOLAR SYSTEM

Cool! So where do we start?

On Earth, of course! We'll begin with a quick intro to the system and a quick *whizz* around the Earth–Moon system. Then after that it's up to you.

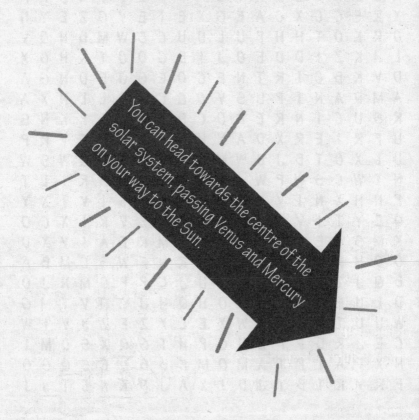

You can head towards the centre of the solar system, passing Venus and Mercury on your way to the Sun.

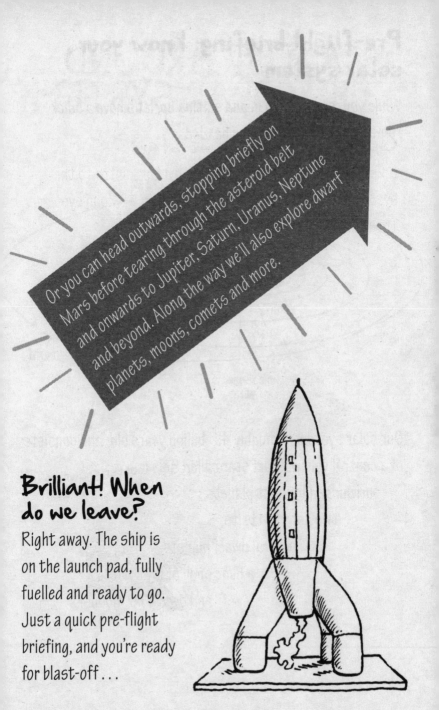

Or you can head outwards, stopping briefly on Mars before tearing through the asteroid belt and onwards to Jupiter, Saturn, Uranus, Neptune and beyond. Along the way we'll also explore dwarf planets, moons, comets and more.

Brilliant! When do we leave?

Right away. The ship is on the launch pad, fully fuelled and ready to go. Just a quick pre-flight briefing, and you're ready for blast-off . . .

Pre-flight briefing: know your solar system

While you're strapping in and suiting up, let's have a quick run-through of where you're headed.

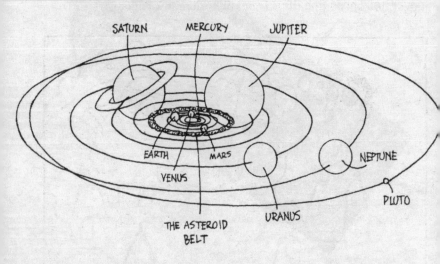

SATURN MERCURY JUPITER

EARTH MARS

VENUS

NEPTUNE

PLUTO

THE ASTEROID BELT

URANUS

Our solar system is roughly 4.5 billion years old, and consists of a central yellow dwarf star called Sol **(better known as the Sun)** surrounded by eight planets,

two asteroid belts,

several dwarf planets,

a huge shell of icy comets

and over **170** moons!

A hundred and SEVENTY moons? Wow!

Yep. If you had a fast enough spaceship, you could visit a different one every year for your summer holiday, and still never get through half of them in a whole lifetime.

And what's a dwarf planet?

It's a large, rounded object that is much bigger than an asteroid or comet, but not quite big enough to qualify as a planet. Unlike moons, dwarf planets orbit the Sun directly, rather than orbiting other planets. There are at least five of them in our solar system, the most well known being Pluto. But there are probably at least forty or fifty more. We'll learn more about dwarf planets later.

So, are you ready to go?

Almost. One more thing: how did we figure all this stuff out? Like, how long a Martian year is, and how cold it is in winter?

Well, as we saw in Chapter 2, Johannes Kepler figured out that the path and speed of a planet's orbit depends upon how far away it is from the Sun, and Isaac Newton later worked out that this, in turn, depends on how **big** the planet is. That's why the four small planets known as the Terrestrial planets (Mercury, Venus, Earth and Mars) orbit close to the Sun, while the more massive Jovian planets (Jupiter, Saturn, Uranus and Neptune) orbit at much greater distances.

Get it Sorted – Planets	
TERRESTRIAL PLANETS	**JOVIAN PLANETS**
Mercury	Jupiter
Venus	Saturn
Earth	Uranus
Mars	Neptune

Cool! OK – I'm ready now. Let's go.

Roger that. Countdown commencing.

First stop:

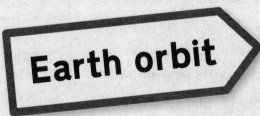

3 . . . 2 . . . 1 . . . **lift-off!**

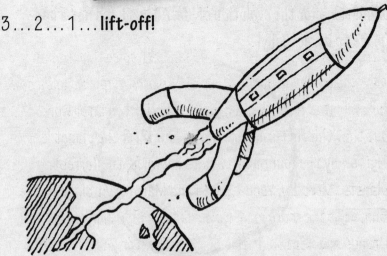

THE EARTH-MOON SYSTEM

There's no place like home.

What makes the Earth so special?

Oooh, lots of things.
It has water in all three forms —

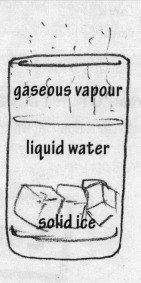

gaseous vapour

liquid water

solid ice

It has a magnetic field and ozone layer that shield its surface from harmful radiation. It has the perfect range of temperature, pressure and other atmospheric conditions for the evolution of life. All in all, it's not a bad place to be, actually!

For obvious reasons, we know more about the Earth and Moon than any other part of the solar system. After all – these are the only two bits of it we've ever actually set foot on.

The Earth is a rocky ball around 8,000 miles (12,700 km) wide at the equator. It spins on a central axis that runs through the north and south poles, tilted at a heady 23 degrees from vertical. It rotates once every twenty-four hours, and its spin causes it to bulge around the middle, so it's almost – but not quite – a perfect sphere. It is the largest of the Terrestrial (or 'earthly') planets – the four dense, rocky planets that sit closest to the Sun.

The Earth's continents and oceans sit atop a rocky **crust** about 60 miles (100 km) thick, which in turn floats above a semi-solid **mantle** of molten rock 1,800 miles (3,000 km) deep. Beneath that lies a

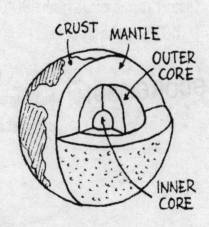

liquid metal **outer core**, and a solid metal **inner core** – both made mostly of iron and nickel.

Earth's breathable atmosphere

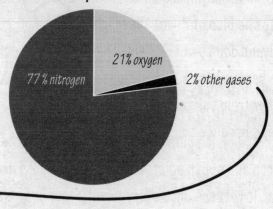

77 % nitrogen
21% oxygen
2% other gases

Among these, **water vapour** cycles life-giving water between the seas and land, while **carbon dioxide** and other 'greenhouse' gases help reflect heat back towards the Earth, keeping it much warmer than it would otherwise be. Surface temperatures range from –90°C (–130°F) at the icy poles

BRRRRRRR

SCORCHING!

to 60°C (140°F) in the deserts... but the average is a toasty, comfortable 15°C (60°F).

Doesn't that change with the seasons too? Why does that happen?

The seasons change as the Earth moves through its year-long orbit around the Sun, exposing the northern and southern halves (or hemispheres) of the planet to more or less sunlight at different points of the orbit. This is not — as some people think — because the Earth is closer or further from the Sun at these times. It's because the Earth's axis is always tilted the same way, and doesn't rotate as the Earth spins and orbits the Sun.

Well, it does. But it takes about 26,000 years, so most of us don't notice the effect.

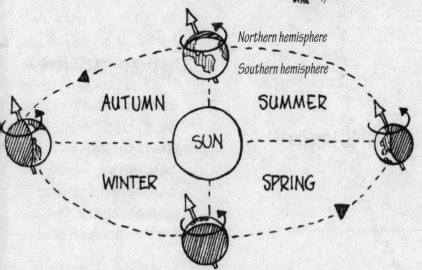

Northern hemisphere

Southern hemisphere

AUTUMN

SUMMER

SUN

WINTER

SPRING

It's this ideal pattern of heating and cooling, together with its precise distance from the Sun, which makes the Earth so special, and such a superbly unique place for supporting life in the solar system.

The planets closest to the Sun have no water. They are so hot that all of their oceans have boiled off.

THE SUN

The Earth is at the right distance from the Sun, and therefore the right temperature, to keep water in all three forms. So it has solid ice at the poles and on mountain tops. It has liquid water in its oceans, lakes and rivers. And it has gaseous water vapour in its atmosphere (which condenses into liquid droplets in clouds, and falls to earth as rain or snow).

Why is the distance so important?

Well, at the birth of the solar system, the distance from the Sun at which each planet settled into orbit ultimately decided how hot it would be. This, in turn, affects the nature of its atmosphere, oceans (if any) and weather systems.

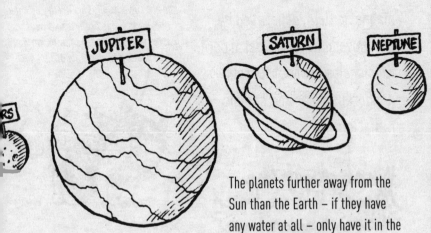

The planets further away from the Sun than the Earth – if they have any water at all – only have it in the form of solid, frozen ice.

So the only thing that makes Earth special is how far from the Sun it is? So, if Mars was a bit closer, it would be just like the Earth?

That's most of it, yes. But it's also to do with how big and dense the planet is. This is because the gases that remain in a planet's atmosphere are held there by gravity. If the gas is too light (or the planet so small that it doesn't have enough gravitational attraction), then parts of its atmosphere 'leak' into Space.

This is why Venus, as we'll see later, has such a hellish atmosphere — the lighter gases slowly leaked away from it, leaving only heavier (and toxic) carbon dioxide and sulphur dioxide gas behind.

The Earth also has a strong magnetic field, generated by the movement of its metal core, which helps protect it from dangerous solar and cosmic radiation.

In fact, this is even happening to the Earth. We're leaking hydrogen into Space too — just a great deal slower than Venus has been. Eventually this will dry up entire oceans and drastically affect weather patterns. But it'll take a few billion years, so nothing to worry about just yet!

What about the Moon? We've been there, haven't we? Could we live there too?

Well, let's head up there and find out . . .

ZOOM!

WALKING ON THE MOON

So what's it really like on the Moon?

According to the twelve astronauts who have had the rare privilege to walk on it, the Moon's surface is like a desert — bleak, yet beautiful. It has rocks, boulders, mountains and craters formed by past meteorite impacts. It also has wide, flat plains called maria (from the ancient Latin word meaning 'seas'). Each plain (or mare), it seems, was formed by volcanic lava flows bubbling up from underneath, which spread out to make a smooth, flat surface.

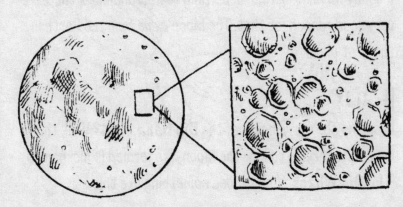

There are volcanoes up there?

There are no active volcanoes on the Moon any more, but at one time there were many. Just like the Earth, the Moon has layers. At the surface is a rocky crust about the same thickness as the Earth's. Beneath that, it has a semi-liquid mantle surrounding an inner and outer core. For 100–150 million years after the Moon was formed, the **churning** mantle was **spewing** molten rock up through holes in the Moon's crust, breaching the surface as lava and creating many volcanoes. But the Moon's volcanoes have long been extinct, as the Moon's interior quickly cooled and stabilized. And the few that now remain are small domes just a few hundred metres high.

Wow. I thought the Moon was just a big rock. With all those mountains, seas and volcanoes, it sounds like it's almost like the Earth.

In many ways, it is. And, according to astronomers, there's a very good reason for that. The Moon *came from* the Earth in the first place.

It did?

It seems so. You've heard of the **Big Bang**, right? Well, the leading theory as to how the Moon was formed is nicknamed '**The Big Whack**'. And it goes something like this . . .

The Big Whack

Around 4.5 billion years ago, when the Earth and solar system were still young, the Earth was just one of several planet-sized objects that were growing and whipping around in the dusty primordial disc surrounding the Sun. Well, one of these objects – a massive asteroid or a dwarf planet, perhaps – whacked into the Earth and smashed a huge chunk out

of it. The resulting debris flew into Space as billions of tonnes of dust and molten rock. This debris was then drawn into a ring around the Earth (much like Saturn's, only those are made of ice, and remain that way – more on that when we get there later on), and eventually clotted together by gravity to form a solid lump.

For a while this new satellite (or moon) stayed molten, and the surface was a fiery place filled with volcanic eruptions and lava flows. Then it started to cool, and after about 900 million years it reached a state which remained more or less unchanged to this day. A cold, crusty ball just over a quarter of the size of the Earth, which circles our planet once every 27.3 days, at an average distance of 240,000 miles (384,400 km).

ASTEROID/PLANETOID COLLIDES WITH THE EARTH...	DEBRIS FORMS A RING AROUND THE EARTH...	WHICH SLOWY BECOMES THE MOON

Is there no air, water or gravity on the Moon, then?

Lacking the size (and therefore the gravity) to keep them there, the Moon has no water, no air and no atmosphere. This also means it has nothing to absorb and hold radiation from the Sun, so surface temperatures range from an ultra-*FREEEEEEZING* −170°C in the shade to a *RRRRROASTING* 130°C in direct sunlight.

The Moon does, however, have gravity. In fact, every object in the Universe does — with a strength that simply depends on how big it is. But, being much smaller than the Earth, it simply generates much less of a pull. At the surface, its gravitational pull is around one-sixth of that of the Earth — which is why the astronauts on those old Moon-landing video clips seemed to bounce around as if they were on wires.

Yeah, but I read something on the internet that said they were on wires. That NASA faked the whole thing. So did we really land on the Moon?

Quite simply — yes, we did. There was no conspiracy, and all the 'proof' the internet nutters put forward is easily explained away if you know anything about physics.

For all the so-called 'proof' these conspiracy theories put forward, every bit of it turns out to be false or misguided. So you can file these fake-Moon-landing theories under 'nutter', along with modern sightings of Elvis and real-life alien abductions.

Landing on the Moon was one of the greatest achievements in the history of humankind. One day, we may go back to explore it further, or even to mine or live on the Moon's surface. So it's a little sad that some people want to mock this wonderful achievement with silly, sneering suspicions. Besides that, there are plenty of interesting (and real) things to find out about the Moon, so why bother mucking about with daft conspiracy theories?

Humans in space – famous dates and highlights

12 April 1961

First one!

Russian cosmonaut Yuri Gagarin becomes the first man in Space, aboard the rocket *Vostok 1*. His capsule circled the Earth once before landing back in Russia.

February 1962

And another!

John Glenn, Jr becomes the first American astronaut in orbit, three years into NASA's Project Mercury programme. His *Friendship 7* capsule was carried into Space by the Mercury Atlas 6 rocket.

March 1965

300 hours!

Russian cosmonaut Alexey Leonov leaves the *Vokshod 2* capsule to complete the world's first spacewalk. A few months later, in preparation for later *Apollo* moon-landing missions, US astronauts Frank Borman and James Lovell, Jr spend over 300 hours in Space (and orbit the Earth over 200 times) learning to manoeuvre and dock their *Gemini VII* craft.

May 1969

Nearly!

Astronauts Thomas Stafford, John Young and Eugene Cernan orbit the Moon aboard *Apollo 10*. The spacecraft's lunar module drops to within 9 miles (14 km) of the Moon's surface for a successful test, but doesn't land.

20 July 1969

Moon landing! Yeah!

Neil Armstrong and Edwin 'Buzz' Aldrin successfully land the *Apollo 11* lunar module on the surface of the Moon (while less-famous astronaut

Michael Collins good-naturedly stays in the orbiter module to make sure they get back OK). In a television broadcast to the whole world, Armstrong utters the immortal words: 'That's one small step for man . . . one giant leap for mankind.' Then he plants an American flag, picks up about 22 kg of moon rock and returns home.

April 1970

Phew!

The ill-fated *Apollo 13* mission almost ends in disaster as an oxygen canister explodes, causing all the spacecraft's systems to fail, and NASA struggles to bring the crew home alive. The three astronauts, James Lovell, Jr; Fred Haise, Jr; and John Sweigert, very nearly suffocate, and barely make it back to Earth after using their landing module as a lifeboat.

11 December 1972

The end . . . ?

Harrison Schmitt and Eugene Cernan become the last men to walk on the Moon, aboard *Apollo 17*. No further landings have since been attempted by the US or Russia (whose accompanying Soyuz programme failed to land even one cosmonaut on its surface).

Why does the Moon change shape?

It's to do with how light from the Sun is reflected off it. Depending on the relative positions of the Earth, Moon and Sun, different parts of the Moon become lit and shadowed. The lit-up parts make the Moon shapes we're so familiar with. Sometimes, of course, the Moon gets right between the Earth and Sun. Then things really get interesting . . .

Hold on – I'm not seeing this. I lost you at 'relative positions'.

OK, so you've noticed that the Moon seems to change shape from week to week – or, if you're looking carefully, from day to day. Right?

Right. Sometimes it's a full circle. And sometimes it's a half-circle or a crescent. Sometimes the left half is lit up, and sometimes the right. And sometimes it even disappears altogether.

You're right, it does. When it vanishes like that, we call it a new moon.

So what's with that? If the Moon's just like a big mirror that circles around us and reflects sunlight, then shouldn't it always be there? I mean, it's not like the Sun can go out. So the Moon can't just disappear.

You're right. The Sun is always there, shining away. And the Moon can't disappear.

But it can *move*. Which means it can also *hide* sometimes.

Eh? What do you mean by that?

Well, we know the Moon circles the Earth every 27.3 days, completing each lap in just under a month. That's much slower than the twenty-four hours the Earth takes to spin on its axis, which is why the Moon (when it's visible) rises and sets, just like the Sun.

But if you think about it, in order for the Moon to *always* be visible, it would have to maintain the same angle to the Sun and Earth year round. So to keep a position behind the Earth at 180 degrees from the Sun (as it does at full moon), it would have to orbit *halfway around the Earth* in the same time it took the Earth to travel *halfway around the Sun*. That would mean the Moon would be orbiting us once a year, rather than once a month.

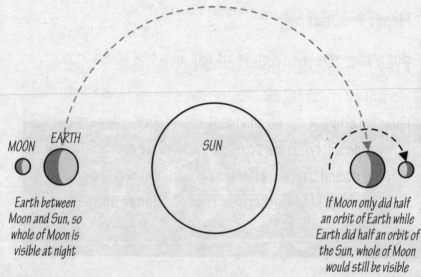

Earth between Moon and Sun, so whole of Moon is visible at night

If Moon only did half an orbit of Earth while Earth did half an orbit of the Sun, whole of Moon would still be visible

Instead, the Moon laps the Earth twelve times faster than we lap the Sun, like an excited puppy running rings around us as we take our slow annual stroll.) Because of this, the Moon's angle to the Earth is constantly changing. So sometimes it's behind the Earth, sometimes it's between the Earth and the Sun, and most of the time it's off to one side.

Remember also that the Moon isn't a flat mirror — it's more like a *mirrorball*. So it only reflects light from the side illuminated by the Sun, and most of the time only part of this lit-up side will be visible to us on Earth. This combination of movement and partial reflection is what causes the changing shapes of the Moon, otherwise known as **lunar phases**.

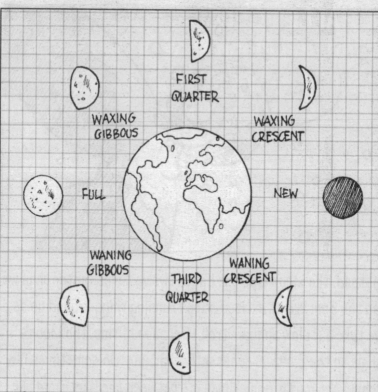

Get it Sorted – Lunar Phases

When the Moon is behind the Earth, fully reflecting the Sun, we see it as a full moon.

When it's between the Earth and Sun, its illuminated side is facing away from us, so we can't see it at all. We call this a new moon.

At right angles to the Earth and Sun, we can only see half of the Moon's lit-up half – hence, we see a half-moon.

And at the angles in between, we see it as a crescent (when less than half of the lit-up surface is visible) or a fat gibbous moon (when between half and all is visible).

CHALLENGE!
Spotting Moon shapes

Tonight, and for the next few weeks, make a quick sketch of what shape the Moon is. Once you have a few weeks' worth of moon shapes, put them together like a comic strip to see how the moon waxes (becomes fully lit after a new moon) and wanes (gradually winks out between full moon and new moon). You'll notice it always waxes and wanes the same way.

Now look again at the diagram opposite and think about where the Moon was relative to the Earth and Sun each time, and what made it that shape. From now on, whenever you look at the Moon, you'll recognize whether it's waxing or waning, and whereabouts it is in Space, relative to the Earth and Sun. Get good at it, and you can even use it as a rough calendar to count the days of the month, just as the ancient astronomers all around the world once did.

Let's see your mates figure all *that* out!

Hang on a minute - I'm confused. If the Moon is right behind the Earth, how can we see it at all? And when it's between the Sun and the Earth, doesn't that make an eclipse?

Well spotted. It does partly disappear when it's *right* behind the Earth (which is called a **lunar eclipse**). And it can cause an eclipse of the Sun (or **solar eclipse**) when it's right in front of it. But most of the time this doesn't happen, because the Moon's orbit isn't in the same plane as the Earth's orbit around the Sun — it's tilted. So the Moon spends most of its time moving above or below the line between the Sun and Earth, and we can see it almost all the time (except for during new moons, as we already saw).

Occasionally, the Moon will cross directly in front of the Sun, causing a solar eclipse. But even when this does happen, it isn't visible from everywhere on Earth — only the places the Moon's shadow passes directly over see a **total eclipse**, while a wider surrounding region may see a **partial eclipse**. During a partial eclipse, the Moon covers part, but not all, of the Sun — making it look as if the Sun is trying to swallow the Moon whole!

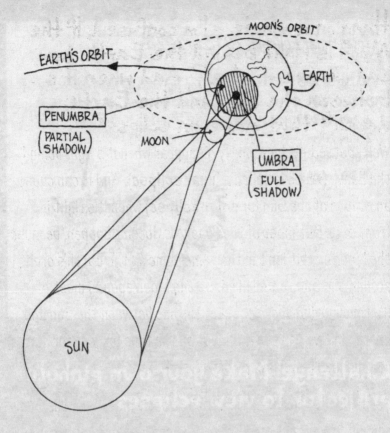

MOON'S ORBIT

EARTH'S ORBIT

EARTH

PENUMBRA
(PARTIAL
SHADOW)

MOON

UMBRA
(FULL
SHADOW)

SUN

Wow! I'd like to see one of those.

If you want to see an eclipse, check the handy chart overleaf for the dates when they will be visible over the next decade. Just make sure you view it properly and safely, as looking directly at the Sun at any time (and especially just before or after an eclipse, when it doesn't seem so painfully bright, so it's easier to stare at) is very dangerous, and can permanently damage your eyes. Instead, follow the instructions overleaf and make your own home-made eclipse-viewer.

Total Solar Eclipses 2013 to 2023

20 March 2015
9 March 2016
21 August 2017
2 July 2019
14 December 2020
04 December 2021

Top Tip! *Check the NASA solar eclipse page (http://eclipse.gsfc.nasa.gov/solar.html) for details of where in the world to see them.*

Challenge! Make your own pinhole projector to view eclipses

All you need is two bits of card — one with a small (1 mm) hole punched through the centre and held up to mask the Sun, the other held beneath. The Sun's image will appear on your DIY projector's 'screen' immediately.

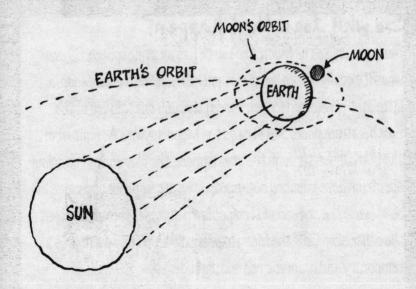

MOON'S ORBIT

EARTH'S ORBIT

MOON

EARTH

SUN

Lunar eclipses

During a solar eclipse, the Moon shadows the Earth. But the opposite can happen too. When the Moon moves directly behind the Earth in the same plane, the Earth shadows the Moon, in what astronomers call a lunar eclipse.

So then the Moon gets blacked out by the Earth's shadow and disappears?

Surprisingly, no. Instead, the Moon turns a deep red colour. This may have been what the writers of the Bible's Old Testament were seeing when they described 'the Moon turning to blood'.

Yikes. That sounds a bit scary.

So why does that happen?

Because, unlike the Moon, the Earth has an atmosphere. So even when it totally blocks the direct path of sunlight to the Moon, a little light is bounced (or refracted) through the thin veil of the Earth's atmosphere and strikes the Moon anyway. As light from the Sun passes through the atmosphere, the blue end of the colour spectrum gets bounced out (making the atmosphere appear blue), while the red end of the spectrum makes it through and out the other side. So if the Moon happens to be in the way, it gets a temporary and dramatic red spotlight.

Being a lifeless object, the Moon does not respond to this with a spontaneous song-and-dance routine, but, during a lunar eclipse, it certainly looks like it should.

Well, now we've whipped around the Earth, learned about atmospheres and seasons, and been eclipsed and mooned by the Moon, that concludes our tour of the Earth–Moon system. So where to next, Captain?

Do you want to head inwards, towards the centre of the solar system? Then turn to page 94 to set a course for Venus.

Venus

Mars

Want to head outwards instead? Then turn to page 120 to set a course for Mars.

VENUS
Earth's evil twin?

If you used enough sunscreen, could you sunbathe on Venus?

I for one wouldn't want to try it. Venus has hellish temperatures, hellish pressures, hellish winds and hellish rainstorms. To summarize: it's pretty hellish. No amount of sunscreen will keep you safe through all that.

Come on. It can't be THAT bad.

Oh, believe me – it is.

Incredibly, astronomers once described Venus as the Earth's 'twin sister' in the solar system. You can understand their mistake. Venus is very similar in size, mass and density to the Earth. If it shared our home planet's orbit around the Sun, it would probably *look* very similar to the Earth too – with oceans and lakes lapping between its rolling hills and rocky landscape, and perhaps even living organisms going about their daily Venusian lives.

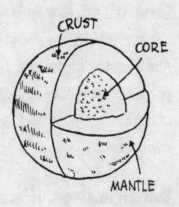

But because of its position closer to the Sun Venus receives far more heat, light and other forms of radiation than the Earth. This stronger 'grilling' has led to huge differences in the interior, surface and atmosphere of the two planets. And when the first Space probe visited Venus almost fifty years ago, we quickly discovered that Venus was no twin of the Earth. Or, if it was, it was an **evil** one with a hellish environment.

What makes it so awful there?

In short, the atmosphere. Unlike the Moon, Venus is large enough to retain a gassy atmosphere with its gravity. But, unlike the Earth, it's not one you'd want to try breathing in.

You may recall that Earth's atmosphere is mostly nitrogen and oxygen, plus a little water vapour, and a tiny amount (less than 1 per cent) of the 'greenhouse' gas carbon dioxide. This keeps the surface temperature on Earth warm and toasty via the heat-trapping greenhouse effect.

Well, on Venus, the atmosphere is over 96 per cent carbon dioxide, less than 3 per cent nitrogen and there's no free oxygen or water vapour at all. Being slightly smaller (and a great deal hotter) than the Earth, the water-forming hydrogen gas on Venus has long since boiled off into Space, while the remaining oxygen became bound to sulphur and other elements.

What remains is just about the worst atmosphere you could ever hope to be in. Clouds of burning sulphuric acid rain down through thick, choking carbon dioxide gas — all held at a pressure ninety times greater than that of the Earth's atmosphere. To make matters worse, the runaway greenhouse effect caused by all the carbon dioxide gives Venus an average surface temperature of around 460°C (850°F).

So what would happen if you landed there and popped out of the spaceship for a stroll?

Nothing good, that's for sure. You'd be squashed flat by the immense pressure, suffocated by the toxic air, roasted alive by the oven-like temperatures and finally

dissolved

by the acid rain. Frankly, not much would remain to indicate that you'd ever been there at all.

Ah. Won't be building our new off-planet home there, then.

Probably not. Even if it wasn't hotter than we could stand, without water or breathable air, there's little hope of maintaining life on Venus, and astrobiologists (scientists who study and seek out extraterrestrial life) have long since given up on finding any native Venusian organisms. But there are a few things that make Venus interesting.

The combined effect of its faster orbit and super-slow backwards spin is that it takes 117 Earth days for any single point on Venus to circle once and face the Sun. In other words, the Venusian day is 117 Earth days long!

Ever feel like a day at school seemed to last for months? Well, if you went to school on Venus, it *would*.

BLAH, BLAH, BLAH...

ZZZZ

Plus it'd be really hot all the time. And you could never go outside to do PE...

Err ... right. Also true.

Like the Moon, Venus also has phases — appearing fully lit, half-lit or crescent-shaped at different times. Galileo (remember him?) first spotted these phases with his telescopes in 1610. This was important, because it provided more evidence for the heliocentric (Sun-centred) solar system — as the different phase pattern to the Moon suggested that Venus (at least) could not be orbiting the Earth.

And, perhaps most importantly of all, Venus gives us a glimpse of what the Earth could look like if the greenhouse effect were allowed to run out of control. Although our atmosphere could probably never get that thick with carbon dioxide, our hellish 'twin planet' stands as a warning of what could happen to our environment if we don't take steps to look after it.

And on that jolly note it's off we go again.

Where to next?

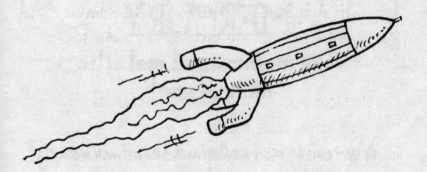

If you're on your way towards the Sun, then turn to page 102 for the innermost planet, Mercury.

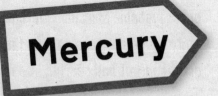

Mercury

Little bits

If you've just come from Mercury and you've now seen all the planets, turn to page 162 for a final whizz through the system to visit the dwarf planets, comets and asteroid belts.

MERCURY
The moon-sized metallic mini-planet!

Is Mercury actually made of mercury?

No, it isn't. Although it is mostly made of metal, the planet Mercury got its name before the metal did. Like most of the other planets, Mercury got its English name from an ancient god in Roman mythology. And as you might expect from a giant red-hot ball bearing, it's not a very inviting place to live.

The pipsqueak of the solar system, Mercury is both the smallest and the closest planet to the Sun. At just 4,800 km across, Mercury is less than half the size of the Earth, and not much bigger than the Moon. In fact, it's actually smaller than several of the moons that orbit Jupiter and Saturn. And with its dusty, crater-faced surface and no atmosphere to speak of, Mercury looks pretty similar to the Moon too. Quite frankly, it's lucky it gets to call itself a planet at all.

Mercury orbits the Sun at a distance of between 47 million and 71 million km, tracing out the most elliptical (or least circular) path of all the planets. But even at its furthest from the Sun, it's still less than half as far from the Sun as the planet Earth. It takes just eighty-eight days to lap the Sun, but rotates very slowly, taking fifty-eight Earth days to complete a single spin on its axis. So if you thought a long school day on Venus was bad, get this — on Mercury, a day lasts for two-thirds of its year!

Had they known this, Aristotle and Ptolemy, with all their love for perfect circles, would have hated Mercury.

Arghhh! That sounds like a nightmare! You'd be doing tests every day. Plus it would be even hotter there, right?

Well, not really. But, in fact, it would be even less comfortable going to school on Mercury than it would on Venus. Being much closer to the Sun, you might think that it would be much hotter. But while surface temperatures on Mercury do climb almost as high (to 450°C, or 840°F) during the daytime, it swings wildly down to −150°C (−238°F) at night. This is because Mercury, like the Moon, lacks an atmosphere to hold the heat. So as soon as it turns away from the Sun, the surface starts to lose heat and freeze.

Although with a day lasting about two months of an Earth year, at least you'd have time to change from your sun-shorts into your Arctic anorak. I'm joking, of course — even with the proper gear, you could *never* survive temperatures that hot or cold.

I knew that. But if you COULD survive the temperatures on Mercury, what would it be like to live there?

Not much more fun than the Moon, I'm afraid. Mercury is basically a barren, pock-marked, rock-covered ball bearing in Space — with a thick core of solid iron and nickel overlaid with a thinner, molten-rock mantle and a crusty surface.

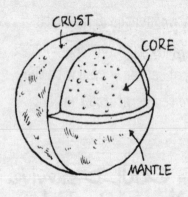

CRUST

CORE

MANTLE

Being larger than the Moon, it has a little more surface gravity, and about a third that of the Earth. So you could do a few high leaps and jumps, I suppose. But other than that there really wouldn't be much to do.

No life, no water, no atmosphere. Not exactly Party Planet Central.

YAWN!!!

Right. That does it. This place is boring. Let's get out of here.

OK. Where to next?

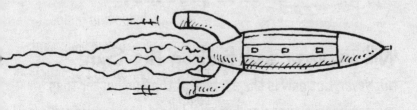

If you're on your way inwards, towards the centre of the system, then grab your shades and tanning lotion, and turn to page 108. Next stop: the Sun.

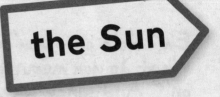
the Sun

Venus

If you've just come from the Sun and you're heading out to see more, turn to page 94 to explore the planet Venus.

THE SUN

Is it getting hot in here, or is it just me?

Will we ever set foot on the Sun?

No. Never. Not only is the surface of the Sun hotter than you can possibly imagine, but you'd most likely never make it through the Sun's outer halo to reach it. And even if you did, there would be nothing to stand on.

Eh? Hold on – you've lost me there. What do you mean 'nothing to stand on'? And since when did the Sun have a halo?

OK, let's roll this back a bit. First, here's the lowdown on the Sun itself. Strange as it may seem, the only true star of our solar system is a middle-aged dwarf.

NO... NOT THIS KIND OF DWARF!

What?

I'm serious. The Sun (it has no official astronomical name, but is sometimes given its ancient Roman name, Sol) is a class-G yellow dwarf star that is roughly 4.6 billion years old, which puts it a bit under halfway through its estimated 10-billion-year lifespan. Compared to other stars, such as blue supergiants, the Sun is fairly small, and not that hot or bright. But when you try to get your head around the sizes and temperatures involved, you soon see that the Sun is no less impressive for that.

STARS

Stars are basically huge balls of gas and dust held together by the force of gravity. They're formed as massive gas-and-dust clouds are pulled together under their own gravitational attraction, which triggers a series of reactions and transformations that eventually result in a star.

Like everything else in the Universe, stars are born, grow up, grow old and eventually die – or at least pass on into another form. Gas clouds of different sizes form stars of hugely different sizes, types and temperatures. These burn away in Space for a long (but limited) time. Then eventually they will collapse

STARS FORM IN A NEBULA, FROM COLLAPSING CLOUDS OF INTERSTELLAR GAS AND DUST...	THE STAR BURNS HAPPILY THROUGHOUT ITS LIFE...	UNTIL, AT THE END, IT BEGINS TO EXPAND INTO A RED GIANT...
ONCE ALL THE GASES HAVE BURNED AWAY...	ALL THAT'S LEFT IS WHAT'S KNOWN AS A WHITE DWARF	AS THIS COOLS, THE STAR THEN BECOMES A BLACK DWARF

Stars are classed by temperature and further sorted by brightness (known to astronomers as **magnitude**). There are seven basic classes of star which also correspond to certain ranges of size, temperature and colour. This happens because the biggest stars also have the hottest atmospheres, and the hottest stars burn with different colours to the cooler ones. For example a class-O star, which is about 16 times bigger than the Sun and about 5 times hotter, is blue, whereas a class-M star, which is about half the size of the Sun and about half as hot, is orange or red.

BIG NUMBERS ALERT!

The Sun contains 99.85 per cent of all the mass in the solar system, weighing in at roughly 2×10^{27} (or 2,000,000,000, 000,000,000,000,000,000) tonnes.

Jupiter contains another 0.1 per cent, and the remaining 0.05 per cent is split between all the other planets, moons and objects!

It's almost *impossible* for us to imagine something as massive as this. On a giant pair of weighing scales, you'd have to put 330,000 Earths on the other side to balance it out. But because the Sun is four times less dense, it would take up a great deal more space. In terms of volume, you could fit roughly 1.3 million Earth-sized planets inside the Sun. So, in a way, the Sun is very heavy, but also very big and fluffy . . .

The Sun is also the source of heat and light in the entire solar system, belting out around 4×10^{26} (or 400,000,000,000, 000,000,000,000,000) Watts of power – equivalent to *400 trillion-trillion* lightbulbs!

Whoa That's pretty hefty. So how hot does it get?

Well, that depends on which bit of the Sun you're talking about. Unlike the rocky planets, the Sun doesn't have strictly separated layers, as its gassy structure kind of blends them together. But for convenience astronomers divide the 'body' of the Sun into three major zones. At the 'surface' layer, called the photosphere, temperatures reach about 5,500°C (10,000°F). In the convection zone beneath, they reach 2 million °C (3.6 million °F). Beneath that lies the radiative zone, and temperatures there reach up to 7 million °C (12 million °F). And right in the centre of the Sun, within the fusion core, it may reach 15 million °C (27 million °F) or more.

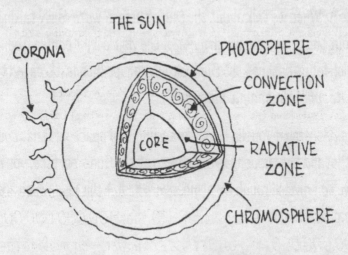

THE SUN

CORONA

PHOTOSPHERE

CONVECTION ZONE

CORE

RADIATIVE ZONE

CHROMOSPHERE

So you could never walk on the surface, not even if you had a special sun-proof suit or something?

Almost certainly not, I'm afraid. Even the strongest heat-proof suits (the kind that some volcano researchers and firefighters wear) only protect you up to about 1,000°C (1,800°F), so would melt away the instant you set foot in the photosphere. Not that you could actually 'set foot' on the Sun, either. Being a giant gas ball, the Sun has no solid surface to stand on, so if you tried you'd fall right into it. When we talk about the Sun's 'surface' we're really talking about the layer from which most of the visible light comes from, which for us outlines the Sun's circular shape (hence it's called the *photosphere*, meaning 'light-ball').

Besides, even if you did have a spaceship and spacesuit that could withstand the thousands of degrees at the Sun's 'surface', you'd have to travel through its atmosphere first — parts of which are a great deal hotter.

The Sun's halo

The Sun's atmosphere extends for 6,000 miles (10,000 km) or more into Space, and has two layers — the chromosphere and the corona. Both contain a range of gases at low densities, and both are normally invisible to us down here on Earth, appearing briefly only during an eclipse. This is because the photosphere beneath is much, much brighter, and outshines the dimmer atmosphere. But when the Moon temporarily shades out the photosphere during a total solar eclipse, the chromosphere and corona appear as a beautiful, fiery halo.

MORE BIG NUMBERS!

The chromosphere ('colour-ball') extends 1,200–1,800 miles (2,000–3,000 km) from the Sun's surface, and temperatures here range from 4,000–8,000°C (7,000–14,000°F). Outside this, the corona ('crown') is more wild and variable. Huge flaming spikes (or spicules) formed in the photosphere project through it and extend for 3,700–6,200 miles (6,000–10,000 km) into Space, whipped up by shifts in the Sun's immense magnetic field. Temperatures in this outer layer of the atmosphere can reach over 1 million °C (1.8 million °F) – over a thousand times those on the Sun's surface.

Spinning Sun

Believe it or not, the Sun spins, just like the planets do. It completes about one turn on its axis each month, but, unlike the more solid planets, different parts of the Sun rotate at different speeds. At the equator, a full lap takes twenty-five days, but nearer the top and bottom, it takes more like thirty-six days. It's doing a gigantic twist, leading from the middle.

Remember – unlike the rocky planets, the Sun isn't a solid ball. It's more like a huge, 3D whirlpool in Space – only it's made of gas instead of water.

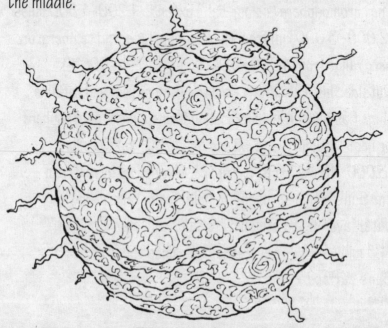

But it always looks the same to me. I've never seen the Sun spin or twist . . .

Ah, but astronomers have. **Galileo** was one of the first astronomers to describe sunspots on the Sun, which eventually clued astronomers in to the movement of its surface. Sunspots are dark, cool patches on the Sun's surface caused by shifts in its magnetic field. By the late-nineteenth century, astronomers had figured out that these spots appeared in cycles, and that tracking their movements upon the surface could reveal its rotation.

Although Chinese astrologers may have observed sunspots a thousand years earlier.

Sunspots also provided visible evidence of the Sun's powerful (but otherwise invisible) magnetic field, which also leads to other strange phenomena like solar wind and solar flares.

What are they, then?

The solar wind is a stream of charged particles which is flung outwards from the Sun by the loops and lines of its magnetic field. The stream of particles whizzes through Space at over 2,200 mph (3,600 km per hour), smashing into objects throughout the solar system. When they hit the icy body

of an orbiting comet, they blast bits of dust and ice from it, creating its beautiful trailing 'tail'. When they reach our planet, they're channelled to the north and south poles by the Earth's own magnetic field. There, they collide with air molecules and create the beautiful, swirling coloured flashes we know as the northern and southern lights. Astronomers called them auroras.

Solar flares are a bit different. These are eruptions of matter from the Sun's surface, which occasionally blast forth from areas close to sunspots when magnetic field lines shift and break. Within a few minutes, a single solar flare can release more energy in the form of heat and charged particles than thousands of nuclear missiles. When flares happen, they cause spectacular auroras on Earth, and may even knock out orbiting satellites and electronic devices. A giant solar flare could, in theory, wipe out all life on the planet – although there's no evidence that's ever happened before, so we seem safe enough.

At our distance from the Sun, flares rarely cause us any danger. But in a spaceship flying within a few hundred thousand kilometres of the Sun itself, we're in serious peril. So let's not hang about.

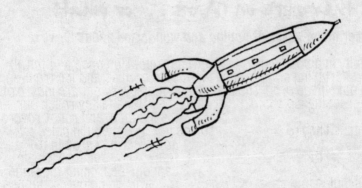

Right. Time to make a swift exit.

Where to next?

If you've already explored the outer reaches of the solar system beyond Earth, then turn to page 102 to zip out to the next-closest planet to the Sun, Mercury.

Mars

Mercury

Otherwise, turn to page 120 to set a course for Mars and beyond.

MARS
Red rocks and robot rovers!

Is there life on Mars . . . or what?

After many years of hoping and wondering about it, we're finally in a position to answer that question once and for all. As satellites orbit the planet and map every square metre of its surface, and robot rovers go careering through its canyons searching for signs of life, we watch, wait and wonder . . .

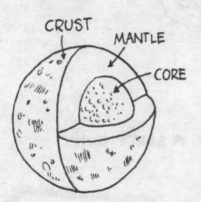

CRUST
MANTLE
CORE

So is there?

Is there what?

Is there life on Mars?

Ah, yes. Of course. 'Is there life on Mars?'

Yeah. So is th—

. . . So sang famous musician David Bowie. Over the years, plenty of people have seemed to think so. In 1863, Italian priest and astronomer Angelo Secchi observed Mars through his telescope and saw pictures of grooves or channels (in Italian, *canali*) on its surface. This sparked a rush of interest in the possibility of Martian life that was to last for many years. In 1894, American astronomer Percival Lowell used his observatory in Arizona to study Mars more closely. From his observations, he mapped hundreds of 'canals' that he thought might have been built by a Martian civilization to transport water from the ice caps to the rest of the planet. By now, the world had Martian fever.

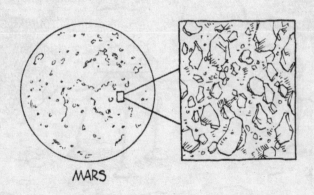

MARS

Grrrr . . . I wish you'd get on with it.

In 1898, H. G. Wells wrote his famous book *War of the Worlds* (more recently made into a movie with Tom Cruise) in

which Martians attacked the Earth using giant war machines. Throughout the 1950s, evil Martians attacked the Earth over and over again in movies like *Invaders from Mars* (1953) and *It! The Terror from Beyond Space!* (1958). Then in 1971, David Bowie asked if there was 'Life on Mars' in his chart-topping song of the same name.

SO IS THERE?

Is there what?

LIFE ON MARS?

Oh. No.

Gaaggh!

Well, certainly not the kind that can build canals and invade the Earth, anyway. And in all likelihood there's no life on Mars at all. Not even a measly patch of lichen on its barren red rocks, or a single, slimy bacterium.

That, frankly, is a bit of a let-down.

Indeed. In fact, the whole history of Mars exploration has been marked with let-downs and disappointments. Here's a summary of the major events (and this isn't even all of them):

Missions to Mars

1960	Mars probe 1960A launched by the Soviet Union. Doesn't even reach Earth orbit.	FAIL.
1960	Mars probe 1960B is launched, four days later. Also wipes out.	FAIL.
1962	The optimistically named Soviet 1962B Mars Lander also fails to leave the Earth.	Again, FAIL.
1964	USA Space probe Mariner 3 attempts Mars fly-by, but fails when solar panels refuse to open. It now orbits the Sun instead, having missed its initial target by roughly 141 million miles (or 230 million km).	MEGA-FAIL.
1964	Mariner 4 passes within 3.7 miles (6 km) of Mars and takes the first close-up photos of its surface.	RESULT!

| 1969 | Mariners 6 and 7 pass even closer, taking measurements and hundreds more pics. Mariners 4, 6 and 7 eventually all end up in orbit around the Sun, presumably to make Mariner 3 feel better about itself. | RESULT! |

1969 Mariners 6 and 7 pass even closer, taking measurements and hundreds more pics. Mariners 4, 6 and 7 eventually all end up in orbit around the Sun, presumably to make Mariner 3 feel better about itself.

RESULT!

1969 Meanwhile, in the Soviet Union, two more Mars probes fail to make it off the launch pad.

FAIL.

1971 The Soviet Mars 2 Orbiter/Soft Lander fails to orbit or land softly, as its rocket-brakes fail and it crashes into the surface of Mars.

EPIC FAIL.

1972 NASA's Mariner 9 Orbiter arrives in Mars orbit during a planet-wide dust storm, but still manages to snap photographs of Phobos and Deimos, the Martian moons, and discovers some new 'river-like' channels on Mars. Although long since inactive, it's still up there orbiting Mars today.

PARTIAL SUCCESS.

1975 NASA's Viking 1 and Viking 2 probes successfully land on Mars, map its surface, take soil samples and search for bacterial life. No life found, but . . .

RESULT!

1992 NASA's Mars Observer fails to observe Mars, as communication with it is lost before it enters Mars orbit.

FAIL.

1996 NASA Mars Global Surveyor makes up for it by getting there and mapping the surface, which it continues to do to this day. This is shortly followed by the Mars Pathfinder – the first successful robot rover to land on Mars.

RESULT!

1998	Japan's Nozomi (meaning 'hope') probe has a communication malfunction before entering Mars orbit. The Japan Space programme literally loses Hope, and cries, 'DA-ME!' ('FAIL!')	FAIL!
1999	NASA Mars Polar Lander is destroyed on impact.	FAIL.
2003	The European Space Agency's Mars Express makes good time to Mars, but its Beagle 2 landing craft fares less well, doing a high-speed face-plant on the surface.	EURO-FAIL.
2004	NASA Mars Exploration Rovers (MERs) Spirit and Opportunity arrive safely on Mars and begin their continuing data-finding joyride around the planet.	SUCCESS!

But Mars is only a bit further away than the Moon isn't it, and we've been there.

Well, we did do a great job getting to the Moon, which was already a very long way to go. But Mars is *much* further off.

Try the exercise overleaf, and you'll get some idea of just how much further.

Make a Scale Model of the Earth, the Moon and Mars

1) Grab a packet of balloons, a golf ball and two friends.

2) Blow up a blue balloon to about 20 cm across, and hold it up in the air.

3) Ask one friend to walk 6 m away with the golf ball, and hold it up. You are holding a model Earth, and your friend is holding a model Moon that is the right size and distance away.

4) If you want to add Mars to your model, then the second friend has to blow up a red balloon to 11 cm across ... and carry it 1,200 m away!

5) Don't be surprised if your friend refuses, and pops the Earth.

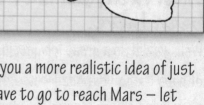

That exercise should've given you a more realistic idea of just how far a spacecraft would have to go to reach Mars — let alone more planets, solar systems and galaxies.

So what's it really like there?

Mars is a dry, dusty desert of a planet. Or rather a *rusty* desert, since its red colour comes from metal oxides on its surface — the same stuff you get on a rusty bike or car.

126

Mars Top Facts

- It's the last of the Terrestrial Planets – the four dense, rocky planets closest to the Sun, the other members of the group being Mercury, Venus and Earth.
- Mars is just over half the size of Earth, and spins on its axis at roughly the same rate – once every 24.6 hours.
- Its atmosphere is a lot more like a chilly Venus than a smaller, drier Earth. Like that of Venus, the Martian atmosphere is over 96 per cent carbon dioxide, together with small amounts of nitrogen and a tiny amount of oxygen. And although it is held at a much lower pressure and temperature, it would still be toxic and unbreathable for humans.
- With surface temperatures on Mars swinging from a toasty 26°C (80°F) to a freezing –125°C (–194°F), it's not the most hospitable place for an extraterrestrial Space colony. But it's not necessarily the worst place for one either.

If we do one day manage to land on Mars and form some sort of base there, the scenery would make it a lot more worthwhile than living on the Moon. Mars has two moons of its own, Phobos and Deimos, plus the largest mountains and canyons anywhere in the solar system.

Olympus Mons, an extinct volcano and the largest mountain on Mars, is 15 miles (24 km) high and 310 miles (500 km) wide. That's over three times taller and wider than Mount Everest on Earth. Alone, it could cover most of southern England, or all of the Hawaiian islands. The great rift valley on Mars, Valles Marineris, dwarfs America's Grand Canyon.

It's over 3,000 miles (5,000 km) long, and up to 62 miles (100 km) wide. On Earth, it would stretch right across the United States.

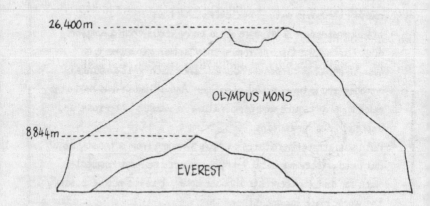

That's pretty cool. But...

But...

...but nothing lives there, and nothing ever has?

Well, we don't know that for sure. According to information recently beamed back by the NASA's Opportunity robot rover, it's too dry and salty on the surface for even bacterial life to survive. But there is evidence — including canyons, ravines and dried-up riverbeds — that water once flowed on the planet. So a long time ago Mars may have been wetter, warmer and a possible home for Martian life. Scientists now think that beneath the Martian ice caps — made mostly from frozen carbon dioxide — there may be massive amounts of frozen water. Some estimate that as much as half of each ice cap may in fact be made of water. If this much water existed, and it somehow melted, it would create an ocean in Mars's northern hemisphere. And maybe, at one time, there was a Martian ocean. Possibly teeming with aquatic Martian life.

But now it's all gone.

As far as we can tell, yes. Mars used to be considered the most probable place to find life (other than the Earth, of course) in the entire solar system. But nowadays astrobiologists are starting to pin their hopes on other places, like Europa (a moon of Jupiter) or Titan (a moon of Saturn).

Well, what are we waiting for?

Eh? What do you mean?

Let's go and look there, then!

Fair enough.

Buckle up – now leaving Mars orbit. Next stop: Jupiter.

Jupiter

JUPITER
The Solar System's Big Daddy.

How many Earths could fit inside Jupiter?

Jupiter is the **giant** of the solar system, being by far the largest planet within it. Jupiter has over **318** times the mass of the Earth, and twice the mass of all the other planets in the solar system combined. But because it's far less dense than the Earth, it's way bigger than 318 Earths in terms of volume. In fact, you could fit about **1,300** planet Earths inside Jupiter's hulking body.

Get it Sorted – Mass vs Density

Density is a measure of how much mass fits into a given volume (shape and size) of an object.

So if two objects with the same mass are different sizes – say, a beach ball and an apple – then the larger object (the beach ball) has less density. On the flipside, the smaller object (the apple) has more density. Get it?

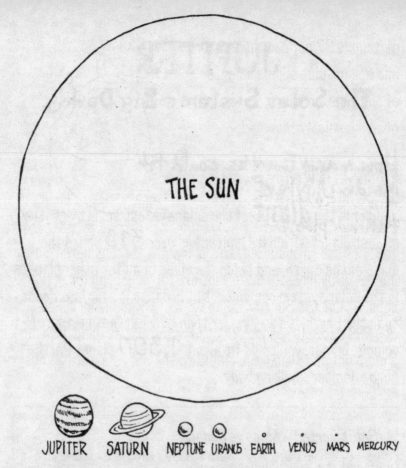

THE SUN

JUPITER SATURN NEPTUNE URANUS EARTH VENUS MARS MERCURY

So Jupiter is way bigger and heavier than the Earth, but isn't quite as solid?

Right. Jupiter is the first of the four Jovian Planets, which are separated from the four Terrestrial Planets by an asteroid belt, and include Jupiter, Saturn, Uranus and Neptune. Like the other Jovian planets, Jupiter is a gas giant — a planet composed more of gas than of solid or liquid rock. It's made of roughly 97 per cent hydrogen and helium, plus small amounts of methane, ammonia, water and other chemical compounds.

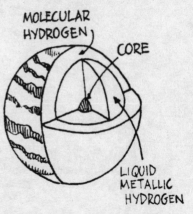

MOLECULAR HYDROGEN

CORE

LIQUID METALLIC HYDROGEN

Weird. That sounds more like the Sun than a planet.

You're right — in many ways, it is. In fact, astronomers think Jupiter probably still looks a lot like the gas cloud (or stellar nebula) that the Sun and solar system formed from billions of years ago — it has just clotted into a sphere and taken on a more defined shape. And, just like the Sun, Jupiter has no surface that you can land on or walk on. The 'surface' we see when we look at it through telescopes is actually just the top layer of clouds swirling above the liquid hydrogen that makes up most of its body.

Jupiter's famous 'red spot' is actually a system of swirling storm clouds — like a permanent hurricane over 40,000 km across. That's almost three times wider than the entire Earth!

However, make no mistake — Jupiter may be gassy, but it's no airy-fairy lightweight. You could fit eleven planet Earths side by side across its equator, and its huge gravitational pull is so

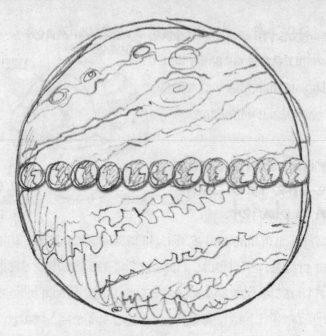

powerful that it affects planets as far away as Mercury and Neptune, and regularly pulls comets and asteroids towards the inner part of the solar system from the vast clouds of rock floating outside it.

In fact, astronomers think that Jupiter's enormous mass shoved most of the planets into place during the formation of the solar system, while preventing other planets from forming at all. If it were not for Jupiter, the asteroid belt might have formed into one or two *more* planets. But then if Jupiter were not there to attract and absorb comets and asteroids, the Earth and other planets probably would have been bombarded with dangerous fireballs far more often.

Does it still pull at the other planets and attract comets now?

Absolutely. In 1994, comet Shoemaker-Levy crashed into the surface of Jupiter after being drawn into orbit around it and ripped to pieces by its gravitational pull. This was the first comet found not to be orbiting the Sun, and showed just how powerful Jupiter's gravity could be.

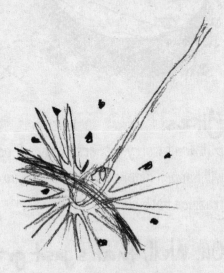

Some astronomers believe that the hulking mass of Jupiter could one day wreck the whole solar system. It is already pulling Mercury into a wider, more stretched orbit each year, and one day it could send Mercury reeling into the Sun (bad), into Venus (worse) or even into the Earth (really not good at all). If this happened, it would destroy all life on Earth, and make previous asteroid impacts look like pinpricks. Both planets would smash into partially liquefied smithereens, leaving very little behind to show that we ever existed.

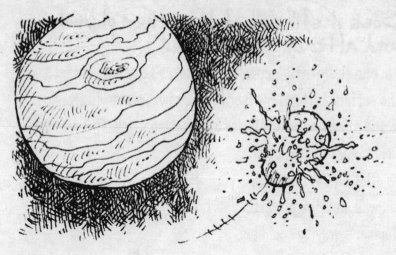

Yikes!

But don't worry — there's only a 1 per cent chance that this will happen before the Sun swells up into a red giant and frazzles both planets anyway.

Oh. Well, that's just great.

Another result of Jupiter's enormous mass is that it has moons. *Lots* of them. **Galileo** spotted the first (and largest) four — Ganymede, Callisto, Io and Europa — way back in 1610. But within the last thirty years, astronomers and Space probes like NASA's Voyager have discovered over fifty more moons, twenty of them discovered between 2001 and 2002 alone! So Jupiter now has sixty-three moons, and still counting.

Him again!

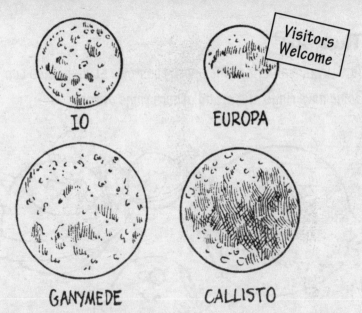

IO   EUROPA

Visitors Welcome

GANYMEDE   CALLISTO

Sixty-three? Wow. So could we make a moon base on one of those? And do any have life on them?

Maybe so. It's certainly possible. Europa, in particular, is a strong candidate for both bacterial life and — in the distant future — manned exploration.

Cool! I like Jupiter. Jupiter rocks.

Here's one more cool thing about it. Jupiter, like Saturn, also has a ring. The Voyager 1 probe discovered this in 1979, when it turned around to take one final snapshot of Jupiter before moving on to Saturn. It came as quite a surprise. But we now know that *all* the Jovian gas giant planets have ring systems.

They do?

Yep. Uranus and Neptune sport their own stylish rings too. Some have rings of ice, and others rings of rock.

But none, perhaps, are as impressive as the rings of Saturn. It's also, coincidentally, where we're off to next. So buckle up cos we're off to the 'planet with the bling'.

Saturn

SATURN
Giant with a halo . . .

What are Saturn's rings made of?

Ice and rock, clustered
beautifully into
circular rows and
lanes, which are
helpfully held in place
by the orbit of Saturn's
'shepherd moons'.

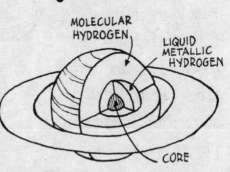

MOLECULAR HYDROGEN

LIQUID METALLIC HYDROGEN

CORE

Saturn's rings have fascinated astronomers
for centuries since the time of **Galileo**.

(again!!!)

But only recently, after sending Space probes to take a closer look,
have we come to understand how and why they formed.

So Galileo spotted them first?

Right. But he couldn't explain what he was seeing.

It's not ears, it's a ring!

Fifty years after Galileo first spotted what he described as 'ears' on the planet Saturn, Dutch astronomer Christiaan Huygens suggested that it was actually a ring around the entire planet, rather than ears, handles or bulges on either side. He also discovered the first and largest of Saturn's many moons, Titan.

The second gas giant in the solar system, Saturn has much the same make-up as Jupiter, and it is almost as large (9.5 Earths would fit across its equator, rather than Jupiter's 11-Earth width). But being much less dense, and lacking the heavier elements in its core, its mass is 'only' about 95 times that of the Earth, compared with Jupiter's 318.

Saturn rotates very quickly on its axis, completing a full spin in just over ten hours, but at its huge distance away, it takes almost thirty years to orbit the Sun.

Never mind all that, what about the rings?

Right. The most stunning features of this planet are, of course, its rings. Seven major rings encircle the planet, stretching to a distance of over 300,000 miles (480,000 km) from the surface. That's over twice the width of Saturn itself, and about 1.5 times the distance from the Earth to the Moon!

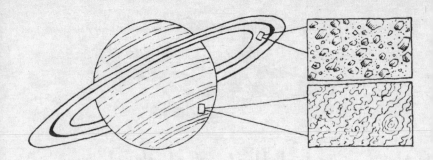

Wow! That's some pretty big bling.

Right. But, unfortunately, these rings aren't made of solid silver or gold. Instead, they're made up of billions of balls of ice or icy rock, ranging in size from microscopic specks to house-sized boulders. And, although it may not look like it, these chunks are so spread out that if you squashed them all together their total 298,000-mile (480,000-km) width could be compressed into a solid ring just a few metres across. It also means that you could easily fly a large spacecraft straight through them without hitting anything.

Smart! I'd love to try doing that.

You'd have to take care, however, not to accidentally hit one of Saturn's moons. Like Jupiter, Saturn has more than sixty of them. Most of these are little more than immense chunks of ice, like dirty snowballs orbiting the planet. But a few, like Titan, Enceladus and Mimas, are more

COOL!

rocky and volcanic (though these volcanoes produce **ice** not lava). Some, like Titan, orbit outside the rings. Others, like Atlas, Prometheus and Pandora, are so-called shepherd moons. These orbit above, below or within the rings — clearing paths between them, sculpting the rings' edges, and helping to hold their shape.

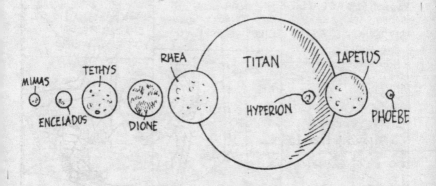

Where did the rings come from? Have they always been there?

We don't think so, no. The rings are very old, but it seems that they may once have been a moon (or a group of several moons) that was ripped apart by Saturn's huge gravitational pull, or possibly disintegrated by the impact of a comet or asteroid.

The rings are made of SMASHED moons? Brilliant!

We think so, yes. It seems that after a moon is broken up like this most of the remaining bits and pieces would naturally be drawn into a ring shape by the planet's gravity, with perhaps some bits coming back together to form new moons later on. That would explain the presence of both moons and rings around Saturn and the other Jovian planets. The Terrestrial planets, however, aren't big enough to create or maintain ring

A MOON GETS TOO CLOSE TO SATURN'S SURFACE AND IS RIPPED APART BY ITS TIDAL FORCES...

THE MOON BREAKS UP INTO ICY/ROCKY CLUMPS, CIRCLING THE PLANET...

WHICH, OVER TIME, BREAK DOWN INTO SMALLER AND SMALLER PIECES... CREATING A RING systems like this. So Earth and Mars may have moons, but they seem destined to remain ring-less.

Shame. So what else do we know about Saturn?

Although a lot still remains to be discovered, NASA's Cassini-Huygens probe, which arrived in 2004, has already revealed more information about Saturn, its rings and its moons than we've ever known before. Among other things, it has spotted oceans, lakes and sand dunes on Titan, icy plumes shooting from cryo-volcanoes on the surface of Enceladus and mysterious 'flying saucers' skimming between Saturn's rings.

Flying saucers? Like, real ones?

Don't get too excited. It turns out they were bits of smashed moon, left behind after moonlets orbiting within the ring system collided.

Oh. Well, that's still pretty cool.

The big draw for astrobiologists, though, is Titan. The atmosphere on Titan is similar to that on Earth billions of years ago, when life here first began. And many scientists now believe that there may be a massive ocean of liquid water beneath its 100-km icy crust. If so, it's possible that alien life of some sort could be lurking within. Maybe some extraterrestrial bacteria, or maybe something more advanced. Who knows?

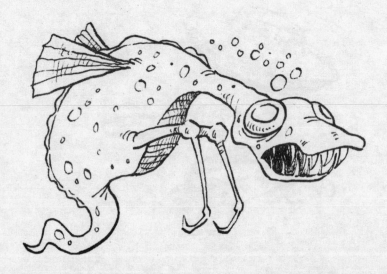

But that's a story for another day. For now, we're off to explore the final two planets in the solar system.

Can we buzz through the rings on the way out? Pleeeeeeeeeeaaaaase?

Oh, all right, then. Here we go.

Wahey!

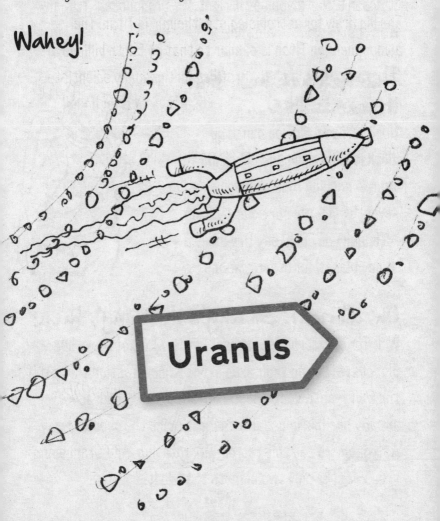

Uranus

URANUS
No one gets my name right.

Why does Uranus sound so rude?

It doesn't. Not if you say it right. It's pronounced 'YOR-ah-NUS', not — well . . . you know.

Heh heh heh heh. But it sounds like . . .

No, it doesn't. So you can stop
all that snickering and chuckling.
There's nothing rude about the
seventh planet in our solar system.
Although you could say Uranus is a
'funny planet' for other reasons . . .

Oh, all right. So why's it 'funny', then?

Well, for starters it spins backwards. Most of the other
planets rotate on their axes in the same direction they orbit
the Sun — anti-clockwise. But Uranus (like Venus, as we've
already seen) is unusual because it spins the opposite way.
Astronomers call this retrograde rotation. And Uranus and
Venus are the only two planets that do it.

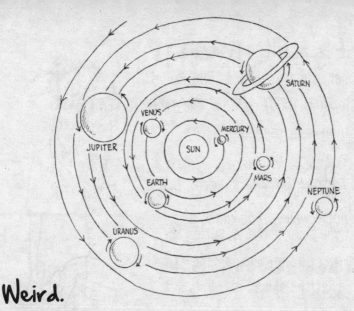

Weird.

It gets weirder. Uranus takes just seventeen hours to rotate once on its axis, which gives it a shorter day than the Earth. But the central axis of Uranus is tilted so far over (at 97.86 degrees, to be exact) it's more or less lying on its side. At one point in its eighty-four-year orbit, its north pole points almost directly towards the Sun. When it reaches the opposite side of the Sun forty-two years later, its south pole points towards the Sun instead. Viewed from above the solar system, Uranus looks almost as if it's *rolling* around the Sun — like a big snooker ball trundling along an invisible groove through Space.

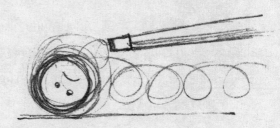

That is a bit strange.

Stranger still, the seasons on Uranus only last for a day. Or rather, the days last for an entire season . . .

Eh? How does that work?

Well, if you think about it, tilting the planet over so that the poles lie flat means that the same bits of planet are exposed to (or shaded from) the Sun even while Uranus rotates. On Earth and the other planets, the planet's vertical spin creates day and night with every rotation, while seasons change as the planet slowly moves around the Sun. But as Uranus 'rolls' its way horizontally around the Sun, half the planet spins away in constant sunlight, while the other half spins in total darkness.

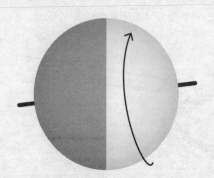

North pole pointing towards the Sun: northern hemisphere in permanent daylight for the whole summer

For day to become night (and vice versa), the planet has to orbit halfway around the Sun, by which time it has also moved through two of the four seasons. And by the time the 'lit' and 'shaded' halves switch back again, another two seasons have passed. So a single day on Uranus lasts for an entire summer, while a single night lasts all winter. How awful would that be?

Oh, I dunno. Not that bad. You could go tobogganing all night long . . .

. . . but then you'd have to get up for school the next day — which would last *all summer*.

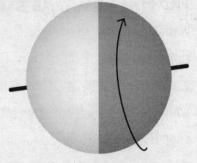

North pole pointing away from the Sun: northern hemisphere in permanent night for the whole winter

Arghhhh!

Exactly. But other than that Uranus is still a pretty cool place. **Cool**, because it's

Cool! mostly made of freezing gaseous hydrogen, helium and water, surrounding a small, rocky core.

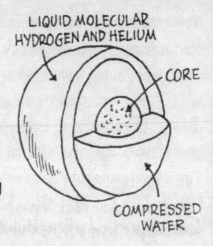

LIQUID MOLECULAR HYDROGEN AND HELIUM

CORE

COMPRESSED WATER

BRRRR icy cool!

<u>Cool</u> because it has a surface temperature which stays at around −200°C (−328°F) all year round.

And <u>**cool**</u> because it also has over twenty-   **COOL BLING!**

five moons and ten rings surrounding it. And just to be different (or awkward, perhaps) the rings on Uranus are vertical, rather than horizontal, like those of Saturn or Jupiter.

Smart! So how did Uranus end up like that? I mean, all sideways and stuff?

Well, as with much of the solar system, we can't say for sure. But many astronomers think Uranus may have been struck a glancing blow by another planet, comet, or asteroid, which bounced its axis of rotation into its current, horizontal state. Then Uranus's satellites (or moons) and ring systems — which at first were probably more like Saturn's — simply followed the lean of the axis and settled into a near-vertical orbit around the planet's sideways-tilted belly.

Wow! It's like a big game of cosmic marbles up there, isn't it?

I guess you could put it that way.

So where do we bounce to next?

That's an easy question. Only one planet left in the solar system.

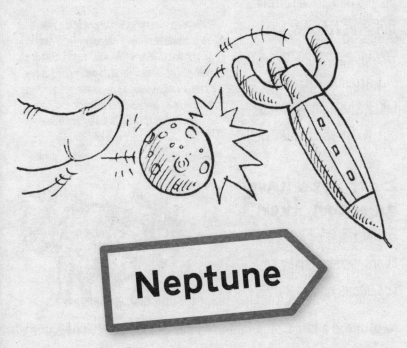

Neptune

NEPTUNE
Deep blue and distant . . .

Why is Neptune called Neptune? Is there an ocean there?

In ancient Roman mythology, Neptune was the god of the seas (the Greeks called him Poseidon). When Neptune was first discovered in 1846, it was given that name because Neptune was one of the few major Roman gods who didn't yet have a planet named after him.

But — as NASA's Voyager 2 probe found out around 150 years later, the name turned out to fit the planet well.

*The other Roman-god planets being **Venus** (the goddess of love), **Mercury** (messenger to the gods), **Mars** (the god of war), **Saturn** (the god of farming) and **Jupiter** (king of the gods). **Uranus**, once again, is the awkward one here — being named after a Greek god, rather than a Roman god. There's always one, isn't there?*

So it does have an ocean, then?

Sadly, no. It's blue, but there its similarity to the ocean ends.

Neptune is a large, blue-coloured gas planet about the same size as sixty planet Earths, but with just seventeen times

its mass. Its colour comes not from a deep blue sea, but from the methane gas in its upper atmosphere. Still, I'm sure Neptune would've been happy to live there. If it wasn't so cold, maybe.

And they didn't know it was blue when they named it?

Nope. Actually, they could hardly see it at all. Before the Voyager 2 probe's 1986 fly-by, we knew almost nothing about Neptune besides the fact that it was ... well ... *there*. Like Uranus, Neptune was invisible to ancient astronomers, as

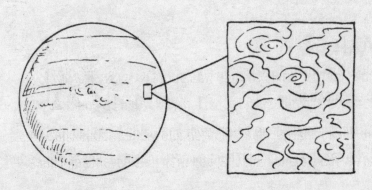

you need a telescope to see it. But unlike Uranus, even *with a* powerful telescope, Neptune is still extremely difficult to see.

So how did they find it, then?
I mean, if you can hardly see it even with a telescope, how did they even know it was there?

They used maths.

Maths?

Yep — maths. While Uranus was spotted by keen-eyed astronomer William Herschel in 1781, even he couldn't make out Neptune with his telescope. That didn't happen until 1846, when French mathematician Urbain Le Verrier did some

sums, figured out where Neptune was and told astronomers where to look for it.

Blimey. How'd he manage that?

He looked at the path of Uranus's orbit, and used Isaac Newton's gravity equations to figure out that something else (other than the Sun, Jupiter and Saturn) must be affecting it. Once he knew something was out there, with a few more swift calculations he also figured out how massive it must be, how far it was from the Sun and Uranus, and quickly calculated its orbit and expected position in the sky. He got it right, to within one degree of where it actually was. Less than three months later, German astronomer Johann Gottfried Galle followed Le Verrier's directions and spotted the real planet Neptune.

That was pretty clever of him.

Yep — very clever. In fact, this was the first planet that was predicted solely using mathematics and only later discovered using real observations. But, ever since, astronomers have been using the same technique to find moons, asteroids and more. They even use it to find planets in other solar systems.

Have they found any moons around Neptune?

Yep. Loads of them. Like all the other Jovian planets, Neptune has multiple moons and rings. Its largest moon is called Triton (who, fittingly, was the son of Neptune in Roman mythology). Triton is an ice-covered planet which — like Saturn's moon Enceladus — is covered with active cryo-volcanoes and geysers that blast ice high into its atmosphere. Many astronomers think there may be liquid water (and possibly even life of some kind) beneath its surface, heated by the planet's hot, volcanic interior. But besides Triton, Neptune has at least twelve more moons, including five that were only discovered within the last decade.

So what's it like there?

Well, as you might expect for the distant outpost of the solar system, it's cold and lonely. Like Uranus, Neptune is pretty much a big ball of ice with a rocky core and a thin atmosphere of freezing hydrogen and helium. Even if you could set foot on its surface, you probably wouldn't want to for long. Like Uranus, its

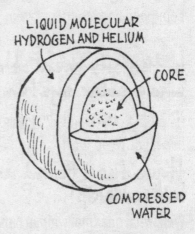

LIQUID MOLECULAR HYDROGEN AND HELIUM

CORE

COMPRESSED WATER

average surface temperature lurks at a bracing −200°C (−328°F). And its cloud systems are made of frozen methane and hydrogen sulphide — which makes the air smell like rotten eggs. Being on Neptune would probably be much like being in a freezer full of farts.

Ugh! Not Pooooeeeeeyyyy!

heading there for my holidays.

I suppose not.

Is that it, then? Have we seen the whole solar system?

Not quite. That's all the planets done, but there's still more to see if you're up for it.

Like what?

Well, with one final whip around the outer reaches and back through the system, we can take in the rarer sights — like the dwarf planets, asteroid belts and comet clouds. How does that sound?

Brilliant! Let's go!

OK. Then buckle up tight — it's full speed to Pluto!

Pluto

SEIDOKU (Planetary sudoku)

Play just like regular sudoku, except the numbers 1–9 have been replaced with the symbols for the Sun and the eight planets in the solar system. It might be tougher than you think! Each horizontal and vertical line – and each square of nine squares – must contain all nine of the following symbols.

Key

Symbol	Name	Symbol	Name	Symbol	Name
☉	Sun	☿	Mercury	♀	Venus
⊕	Earth	♂	Mars	♃	Jupiter
♄	Saturn	⚲	Uranus	♆	Neptune

	♆			⊕				
⚲	☿	♀	♃	♂				☉
♂				⚲		♀		
	⊕	♄		⚲		♆		☿
	♀		☿		♃		☉	
☿		♂		⊕		⚲	♄	
	♄		☉					⚲
⊕				♀	♄	☉	♆	♃
		⊕				♂		

Answers on page 188

DWARF PLANETS
Who'd have thought it?

Why doesn't Pluto get to be a planet any more?

Because astronomers have decided that it's neither big nor unique enough in our solar system. Faced with the discovery of many new Pluto-like objects, they were forced to choose between adding a load of new planets to the system, or calling Pluto and these newer objects something else. Unfortunately for Pluto, they chose option two.

SOMETHING ELSE!

It just doesn't seem right. When did all this happen, anyway?

For thousands of years, there were six planets known to star-gazers and astronomers. In 1781, that six became seven, with the discovery of Uranus. In 1846, seven became eight, with the official discovery of Neptune. Then in March 1930, American astronomer Clyde Tombaugh – after a long and laborious search – discovered Pluto.

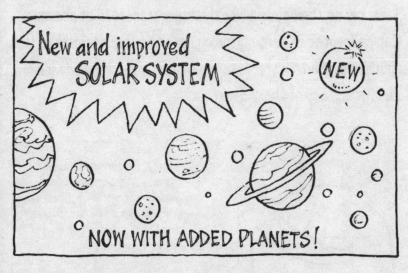

New and improved SOLAR SYSTEM

NEW

NOW WITH ADDED PLANETS!

Pluto is a large ball of ice-covered rock found roughly 3.7 billion miles (5.9 billion km) from the Sun. By comparison, the Earth is roughly five times larger and 500 times heavier, and its surface gravity is twenty times stronger. Pluto takes 248 years to orbit the Sun in an oval orbit so stretched (or eccentric) that it sometimes passes inside that of Neptune.

Shortly after its discovery, it was named by an eleven-year-old British girl called Venetia Burney, whose suggestion was picked from among thousands of others worldwide.

Did she name it after the Disney dog?

Actually, it was the other way around. Mickey Mouse's faithful friend Pluto didn't appear on screen until 1931, a whole year later. So the dog was named after the planet! This little girl knew her mythology and, like the other planets, Pluto's name comes from an ancient mythological character. In Greek mythology, Pluto (otherwise known as Hades) was the King of Hell, or the god of the underworld.

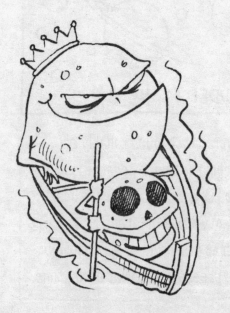

Charon, Pluto's largest moon, was named after the scary skeletal boatman who used to ferry the souls of the dead across the River Styx and into Pluto's underworld. Creepy, eh?

So if it was even smaller than Neptune, how did they find it? More maths, or did someone just spot it one day?

A little of both. Astronomer Percival Lowell (remember him? The guy who thought there were alien waterways on Mars?) He calculated the orbits of the eight known planets, and became convinced that there was another one out there beyond Neptune. He gave it the mysterious moniker 'Planet X', and searched for it using the huge telescope at his own observatory. He died before he could find it, but the task then passed to young astronomer Clyde Tombaugh, who photographed and analysed the positions of tens of

page 121

thousands of stars in his search. Within a year, he had found it. As it turns out, he was very lucky — as Lowell's calculations were wrong, and there was no need for a Planet X to explain the motions of the first eight planets at all.

Well, he wasn't that lucky, was he? After all, his planet's not a planet any more. What's up with that?

Sadly, Pluto wasn't as unique as Lowell and Tombaugh thought. Pluto is just one of many objects orbiting the Sun at roughly the same distance. This is part of the reason why Tombaugh was able to spot it — far from being a mysterious loner, Lowell's 'Planet X' is just one of 200 or more similar objects forming a belt of large, rocky objects beyond the orbit of Neptune.

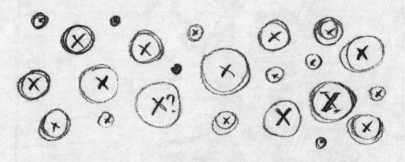

Once astronomers figured this out, they had to decide whether these new 'plutoids', which they were discovering thick and fast, could all be called planets, or whether Pluto, along with these other objects, was really something else. And when astronomer Mike Brown discovered a plutoid (then called Xena, but now formally named Eris) which was *bigger* than Pluto, that pretty much spelled the end of it. Just one year later, in 2006, Pluto the planet was no more, and a new category of celestial object was born. The dwarf planet.

What makes a dwarf planet? Is it just smaller than a regular planet?

Partly, yes. Dwarf planets are a bit more than asteroids and a bit less than a full-on planet. But it's also to do with how and where they're found in Space. If a Sun-orbiting object is spherical (or near-spherical) and massive enough to clear its own orbital path through Space, it's classified as a dwarf planet. If it's smaller, more irregular in shape and exists

alongside other objects in roughly the same path around the Sun, then it's classified as an asteroid or **small solar-system body**. Most — but not all — of the dwarf planets found so far exist in orbits beyond Neptune, in the region of Pluto. These are also known as **Trans-Neptunian Objects (TNOs)** or **plutoids**.

So how many dwarf planets are there?

So far, five have been recognized and named, including Pluto. But there are almost certainly many, many more out there that fit the bill and are just waiting for official naming and recognition.

So what are they called?

The first five recognized dwarf planets **are Pluto, Ceres, Eris, MakeMake** and **Haumea**. Pluto, we know all about already. Here's a bit about the others:

CERES

Ceres, named after a Roman goddess, was previously classified as an asteroid and lies in the wide asteroid belt between Mars and Jupiter. It was discovered in 1801, and recognized as by far the largest asteroid in the solar system. At almost 620 miles (1,000 km) across, it's roughly the same size as France. Its surface gravity is only a fifth that of Pluto, and a thirtieth that of the Earth, but is still strong enough to hold Ceres in a spherical shape. So it looks more like a mini-planet than an asteroid, and fits the dwarf-planet bill nicely.

ERIS

Eris, was discovered in January 2005, and temporarily named UB313, or Xena. At roughly 1,500 miles (2,500 km) across, it's actually a bit bigger than Pluto, so has more right to the dwarf-planet title. It also has it own moon, Dysnomia. Eris sits in an orbit beyond Pluto, around 6.3 billion miles (10 billion km) from the Sun, and takes 557 years to lap it (compared to Pluto's 248-year orbit). It has an atmosphere of frozen methane and nitrogen, giving it a slightly yellowish colour.

MAKEMAKE

MakeMake (pronounced Ma-kay-Ma-kay) was discovered in March 2005, and named after a Polynesian god of fertility. At roughly 1,000 miles (1,600 km) across, it's about three-quarters of the size of Pluto, and sits between Pluto and Eris at an average distance of 4.8 billion miles (7.8 billion km). It takes around 310 years to orbit the Sun.

Haumea was discovered back in 2003, but was more recently reclassified to become the fifth dwarf planet, after much argument and debate among astronomers. It rotates very quickly, which has led astronomers to believe it was once struck by another object, leaving it stretched out and whizzing around the Sun. It's about 1,200 miles (2,000 km) long, but just 620 miles (1,000 km) wide, takes 285 years to orbit the Sun and has two known moons – called Hi'iaka and Namaka.

HAUMEA

Is that all of them, then?

That's all the dwarf planets that have been classified so far. But there are loads more known TNOs and plutoids – including four particularly large ones known as Orcus, Sedna, Quaoar and Varuna – and probably hundreds more out there waiting to be discovered. Some of these may eventually end up being reclassified as dwarf planets too. So the known solar system is expanding every day!

In addition, there are literally millions of smaller objects, such as asteroids and comets, orbiting the Sun at different distances throughout the system. And although they may never reach even dwarf-planet status, they're still important and interesting to study. Not least because some of them threaten to whack into our planet one day . . .

One more question.
What?

Do dwarf planets have, like, dwarfs living on them?
Now you're just being silly.

**Or elves, maybe? No, wait –
then I guess they'd be elf planets . . .**

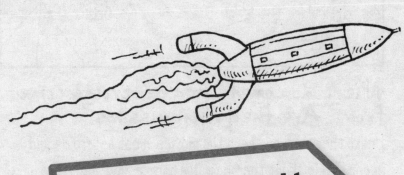

Asteroid belt

ASTEROIDS AND COMETS

Rockin' the solar system!

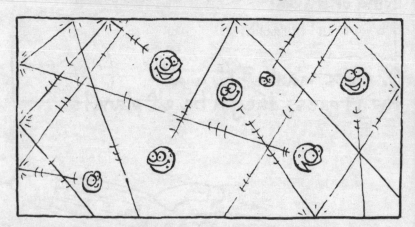

Where do comets and asteroids come from? Are they alien missiles?

Unlike the ones you see in the movies, most asteroids and comets whip about the Sun quite harmlessly. Only some have orbits that intersect with that of the Earth or other planets. And while it's worth watching out for them, we don't have to worry about them ploughing into us and destroying the planet just yet. And no — there's no one flinging them at us.

Are you sure about that?

Yes, pretty sure. Unless you count the planet Jupiter. He does fling them at us from time to time.

Eh?

Let me explain. The vast majority of asteroids in the solar system exist within two wide bands of Space — one between Mars and Jupiter, imaginatively named the

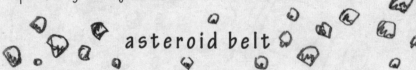

asteroid belt

and the other stretching beyond the orbit of Neptune, in an area astronomers call the

Kuiper belt.

There are millions of asteroids spread between these two belts, but only a small number of them are occasionally pulled or bashed out of their regular orbits, to begin hurtling dangerously towards Earth and the innermost planets.

But aren't asteroid belts dangerous for spaceships and stuff?

Well, since we've never even made it to Mars, let alone beyond it to the asteroid belt, none of our spacecraft has yet had to deal with it. But even when they do, it shouldn't cause too much trouble.

Why not? Won't they have to dodge in and out of the asteroids to avoid getting smashed?

Not really. They'll probably fly straight through. Although there are lots of them, the belt is still so wide that the average distance between two neighbouring asteroids is about **a million miles**.

This is because the gravitational pulls of Mars and Jupiter keep them spread out. So while future astronaut pilots may have to steer occasionally, no last-minute dodging manoeuvres will be needed.

Pah! Bor-ing. So where did all these big rocks come from?

Essentially, they're leftovers, bits of the early solar system that didn't become part of the Sun or planets. Jupiter's massive gravitational pull probably prevented the ones in the asteroid belt from clumping into a dwarf planet, while the rocky fragments in the Kuiper belt are probably too spread out to attract each other at all. So most float alone in Space, with some occasionally being pulled inwards to become Near-Earth Objects (NEOs) and comets.

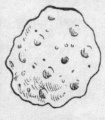

ASTEROID

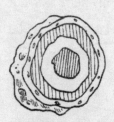

ASTEROID WITH
LAYERED INTERIOR

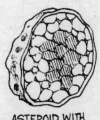

ASTEROID WITH
RUBBLE INTERIOR

Comets come from the Kuiper belt too?

Actually, we think that most of them originate from far further out – from an immense shell of rocky, icy objects that exists far outside our solar system, known as the **Oort cloud**. Most comets spend

most of their time way out beyond the solar system, only being pulled inwards to lap the Sun once every million years or so. A few, however, are captured by the gravity of Jupiter or other planets as they get closer to the Sun, and enter new, smaller orbits within the boundaries of the Kuiper belt. It's these comets that we're typically more familiar with, since they come back around often enough for us to notice. Comet Halley, for example, passes Earth once every 75–6 years, and it's due back in 2061.

Blimey. That's a bit of a wait.

That's nothing. Comet Hale-Bopp – last spotted in April 1997, and probably the most spectacular-looking comet in recent history – is on its way back towards the Oort cloud, and won't be back again until AD 4531. So, if you didn't spot that one the first time, I'm afraid you've definitely missed it!

Famous comets

Name	Orbital period	Last seen	Due back
Halley's Comet, or Comet Halley	75–6 years	1986	AD 2061
Swift-Tuttle	134 years	1992	AD 2126
Hale-Bopp	2,533 years	1997	AD 4531
Hyakutake	14,000 years	1996	AD 15996

What's the difference between an asteroid and a comet, anyway?

Not much — except that comets grow tails as they near the Sun, and generally contain a lot more ice. In fact, these two things are linked.

Comets are basically big, dirty snowballs that orbit the Sun. Close up, as NASA's Deep Impact probe discovered when it smashed into comet Tempel 1 back in July 2005, they look much like asteroids. The nucleus (or centre) of a comet is made of ice and dust surrounded by a rocky crust. When the comet is far from the Sun, this is pretty much all there is to see. But, as it approaches and heats up, the nucleus becomes surrounded by a coma (or body), formed as radiation from the Sun blasts a cloud of ice and dust away from the nucleus. This cloud trails behind the comet as it orbits, creating one of its two tails.

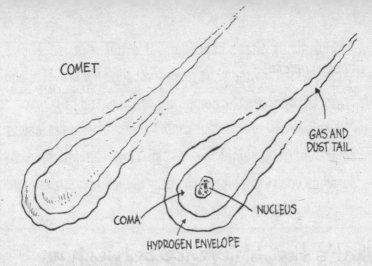

COMET

GAS AND DUST TAIL

NUCLEUS

COMA

HYDROGEN ENVELOPE

Comets have two tails?

Yep. One curving dust tail, and a second, straighter ion tail, which is formed as charged particles (or ions) are swept away from the comet by the solar wind. The effect of this is that the comet looks as if it's whizzing through Space, with its two tails flailing out behind. But, as a matter of fact, the tail doesn't always trail behind the comet at all. It may look that way as the comet moves towards the Sun. But once it has lapped it and is on its way back to the outer solar system, the tail actually trails *in front* of the comet, *leading* its motion.

If you think about what's happening, this makes sense. The radiation and solar wind that form the tails only travel in one direction. So whereas the comet approaches the Sun 'into the wind', it travels away with the 'wind' behind it. So as it leaves the solar system, a comet has its tail 'blown' ahead of it – a bit like when you ride a bike with the wind behind you, and your hair flops forward over your eyes!

Unless you wear a cap or something.
Sorry?

If you wore a cap, that wouldn't happen.
Err ... right ...

But I guess comets don't wear caps, do they?
No. No, they don't.

Pity. That'd be mad cool.

Which would do the Earth more damage – a comet or an asteroid?
That one could go either way. Comets and asteroids are basically just big flying rocks, so it all depends how big they

are, and how fast they're moving. Either one could wipe out all life on the planet, if it was big enough. But, thankfully, that doesn't happen too often.

OK – give it to me straight. Will a comet or asteroid destroy the Earth one day, or what?

Well, even the largest comet or asteroid couldn't *destroy the planet*. The planet Earth is just too big. But a big enough impact could destroy most or all of the *life* on Earth, yes.

Yagghhh!

And impacts like this aren't unheard of, either.

Yaaagghhh!

As recently as 1994, Comet Shoemaker-Levy smashed into Jupiter after breaking into several pieces, leaving scars on it for months afterwards. If just one of those larger fragments had struck the Earth, rather than Jupiter, it would have killed everything on the planet except maybe bacteria.

Plus, the material blown into Space by the impact would have given us a second moon. Which would've been nice, if only there were people left alive to enjoy it!

Great. What about asteroids?

Large asteroids have probably struck the Earth and caused mass extinctions at least twice in the Earth's history, but we haven't had a biggie for a while. The last large object to strike the Earth (technically it exploded above the ground, but you get what I mean) was the Tunguska meteoroid, which exploded over Siberia in 1908 with the force of a nuclear bomb. Thankfully, it didn't destroy anything beyond a few thousand trees in the forests beneath. But a similar-sized asteroid 'buzzed' the Earth in March 2009, missing us by just 44,000 miles (70,000 km) — a mere whisker in Space terms.

That one's due back in March 2067, and looks on course to miss again. But there are plenty of other NEOs lurking out there, and it's probably just a matter of time before a big-un whacks us.

Yaaagghhhh!!!

That's not very good, is it?
So what can we do about it?

Astronomers and space agencies worldwide are already working to locate and track as many NEOs as they can, in an effort to figure out which ones may pose a threat, and give us as much advance warning as possible before it happens. Much of this is part of the NASA Spaceguard project, which was kicked off in 1992 with a goal of mapping at least 90 per cent of the NEOs up there within ten years.

Beyond that, we're also trying to figure out how we'd deal with it if we found out a comet or asteroid was going to hit us soon.

Idea one: blow it up

We probably wouldn't be able to blow a big one up (at least not without creating a bunch of equally dangerous fragments).

Idea two: blast it off course

This could work, while it's still some way off in Space.

Idea three: attach a 'Space Sail'

The sail would use solar wind to blow the asteroid off course. COOL!

The good news is there are no signs of any dangerous asteroids or comets just yet, and it may be thousands of years before there's another impact big enough to cause massive, planet-wide extinctions.

But what happens if we do find one that big? What then?

Well, if we spot it in time, and provided we have the technology, one final option could be to hop the planet and live in Space, or colonize another planet or moon.

This brings us to the end of our tour of the solar system. Now we leave the asteroid belts and comet clouds behind, and we're on our way home.

That's good. I'm hungry, and I could use a bath.

You're telling me.

What?

Nothing.

Hmmmm.

Now go and change your socks and underpants. *Please.*

Build a solar system!

Group the twenty items into the five correct categories.
Draw lines between category and item.

Categories	Items
	Ceres
Terrestrial planet	MakeMake
	Mars
	Halley's
	Titan
Jovian planet	Jupiter
	Uranus
	Shoemaker-Levy
Moons	Mercury
	Eris
	Charon
	Neptune
	Hyakutake
Dwarf planet	Saturn
	Earth
	Pluto
	Venus
Asteroid/comet	Europa
	Hale-Bopp
	Ganymede

Answers on page 188

ANSWERS

Astronomer wordsearch from page 61

K	U	S	K	F	Z	J	H	Y	C	A	B	N	D	F	V	N	J	K	A
X	R	F	C	C	X	C	A	E	G	X	E	T	E	V	G	Z	E	Y	H
O	R	K	O	T	H	H	P	U	L	U	U	C	S	W	M	B	N	Q	V
L	H	K	Z	I	D	D	E	O	J	I	B	G	O	O	T	K	H	O	X
D	V	K	B	C	I	R	T	N	E	C	O	E	G	O	E	O	N	G	A
A	M	D	A	N	T	P	U	S	V	C	Q	C	H	D	L	L	N	X	A
R	S	U	C	I	N	R	E	P	O	C	D	L	E	R	T	P	K	N	S
U	F	R	I	E	R	X	D	A	Y	H	W	F	K	N	O	T	V	R	P
U	L	X	O	T	B	J	B	W	M	U	H	V	E	S	T	Q	W	S	W
N	T	W	C	S	W	P	W	J	E	I	X	T	P	N	S	R	I	L	T
P	N	H	X	N	I	V	Y	H	L	O	W	K	L	S	I	V	I	X	Y
Q	E	Y	T	I	V	A	R	G	O	X	B	D	E	V	R	I	X	C	O
K	M	S	C	E	I	R	B	N	T	I	I	M	R	F	A	I	V	X	D
O	D	H	P	K	P	Z	N	C	P	H	R	N	F	W	S	C	M	B	A
B	Q	J	T	I	F	E	Z	C	J	U	J	C	P	P	O	M	N	J	O
D	L	U	E	O	L	U	X	J	O	H	Q	H	U	M	Q	V	T	M	G
W	U	U	T	R	N	L	Z	W	X	E	L	X	Z	E	Z	J	V	I	W
C	E	J	R	B	F	P	E	U	G	P	H	T	G	Q	X	S	D	M	I
N	X	F	A	I	P	T	A	M	Q	M	C	B	B	U	E	S	Q	G	O
F	R	V	R	T	B	Y	J	D	I	X	A	J	D	K	K	C	T	J	I

Seidoku from page 161

♄	♆	♃	♀	☉	⊕	☿	⛢	♂
⛢	☿	♀	♃	♂	♆	♄	⊕	☉
♂	☉	⊕	♄	☿	⛢	♃	♀	♆
☉	⊕	♄	♂	⛢	♀	♆	♃	☿
♆	♀	⛢	☿	♄	♃	♂	☉	⊕
☿	♃	♂	♆	⊕	☉	⛢	♄	♀
♀	♄	♆	☉	♃	♂	⊕	☿	⛢
⊕	♂	☿	⛢	♀	♄	☉	♆	♃
♃	⛢	☉	⊕	♆	☿	♀	♂	♄

Build a solar system! from page 187

Terrestrial planets: Mercury, Venus, Earth, Mars.

Jovian planets: Jupiter, Saturn, Uranus, Neptune.

Moons: Titan, Ganymede, Europa, Charon.

Dwarf planets: Pluto, Ceres, Eris, MakeMake.

Asteroids/comets: Hyakutake, Halley's, Shoemaker-Levy, Hale-Bopp.